THE LONER GIRL IN LONDON

2011 & 2012

ON BEING
BOOK IV

J. GUZMÁN

For permissions and collaborations contact: j@jguzman.space

You can connect with J. on Instagram @jguzmanwriter, or visit her website https://jguzman.space

Sign up for J.'s newsletter called *Nothing I Say is True: Open Letters to Void* at her website under the "Correspondence" tab! There you can read her ongoing musings about life, the universe, and whatever the fuck.

Although the following narrative is of events that actually occurred, the story itself is only subjective truth. All books in the series *On Being* are J. Guzmán's personal experience, interpretation, opinions, and feelings, not the Objective Truth of Absolute Reality. Her aim is not defamation and she understands that every character has their own subjective truth regarding events that occurred, and that others' perspectives could prove contradictory to her own. Characters' names have been changed to protect their privacy and reputation.

Preface

The Loner Girl in London is volume 4 of the series *On Being*. It contains the last third of the protagonist Ana's year 2011 and all of her year 2012. Subsequent publications will include only one year of Ana's life.

You do not have to read *On Being* by starting at its beginning to understand what's going on, but if you do you will get a clearer and more linear view of Ana's life. *On Being* is an astrological, metaphysical, self-referential, self-psychoanalytic case history. It is meant to serve Astrology as a true, scientific tool one can use to understand the multiverse and Energy in a more profound way, by providing the raw data necessary for astrological analysis. An in-depth explanation of what that entails can be found in the introduction to the series at https://jguzman.space. The same introduction is at the beginning of *The Thought Thinker is a Loner Girl* (volume 1 of *OB*).

Undated entries in volume 4 were taken from sketchbooks and small notebooks of random musings that Ana didn't attach a date to. I've tried to correctly and accurately place them into the chronology but it's not perfect.

If you find Ana's life and perspective intriguing, you can get a glimpse into her current state of mind by signing up to *Nothing I Say is True:*

Open Letters to Void by visiting the website above and clicking on the "Correspondence" tab. I, J. Guzmán, am your Ana, and *Nothing I Say is True* is my newsletter. If you'd like to contact me about anything or respond to my open letters, please do! The best way is to sign up for the newsletter. If you don't want to, simply email me at j@jguzman.space or find me on Instagram @jguzmanwriter.

Some notes on Ana's astrology for the years 2011 and 2012: Ana is 20 years old in 2011, which means that she's in a 9th house profection year according to annual profections. This would highlight Libra and thus Venus for the year. However, as she has a 12th house Capricorn stellium with both luminaries there, one could make the case for profecting from the 12th, which would put her in an 8th house Virgo profection year ruled by Mercury. Maybe both are valid. For 2012, as a 21-year-old, profecting from the 1st would put Ana in a 10th house, Mars-ruled, Scorpio year, and profecting from the 12th would be the 9th house Libra and Venus emphasis. Which houses do you think have more emphasis and are more activated for each year?

Something else I would like to mention before you start reading: I don't like how this book was written, and I don't like who Ana was when she wrote it. If she had known about astrology and that she was writing a case study, she would have written more often and included many more details. So much of what happened is missing. But, alas! Here we are. This is what happened, and the point of *On Being* is to document Ana's truth as it evolves throughout Time. The truth requires no editor. Ana won't discover astrology until book 8.

Also, just as a general human being, she kinda sucked. Not a good friend, vaguely and sometimes overtly alcoholic, wielding sex as a weapon and wounding herself in the process. She was deeply insecure and confused, and thus exhibited a general air of disregard and disrespect towards others and herself. It makes sense though, when you realize Neptune was square her Mars the whole time.

–J.

May/June 2023
Boise, Idaho, USA

P.s. For the astrological analysis, remember Ana’s birth info is as follows:

January 14, 1991
8:42 a.m.
Lewiston, Idaho, USA

the loner girl in London

2011 & 2012

03 August 2011

A list: spools of thread, fingernails, caffeine, fruit, doubt, hierarchies of importance, slanted writing, not being sure what to expect, night, thoughts, history, planets, other planets, grime, alcohol, feelings of well-being, remembering that people love you, parties, genuineness, photographs, yarn, first impressions, learning something new, colors, seasons, words, painting, tile, showers, siblings, religions,

anticipation, pills, feathers, hair, love as a swirl of emotion, waiting, music as a representation of emotion, flying, chai tea, daydreams, normal dreams, creating scenes in your head at night, connections between people, pessimism, romance, (pessimism = romance), deodorant, sleepiness, movies, daylight, blankets, swimsuits, glow from the setting sun, fields of wheat or flowers or grass, meadows, the smell of Sharpie, socks, packing,

reading between the lines,

traveling, kissing, writing, holding, markets, grocery stores, lipstick, cigarettes, running, bicycles, talking, smiling without teeth, baldness, money, blood, silverware, plans, doors, pencils, phones, keys, pages, documenting thought processes, hope as a bullshit concept, school, street smarts, dishwashers, closets, clothes, selling your clothes, eating, walking, exploring, adventures, satellite dishes, internet, the thinning of the atmosphere the higher you rise, hating your life, yearning, longing, cutting,

scissors, shaving, bedrooms, lunchboxes, elementary school, happiness, the nonexistence of anxiety, waking, desperation, driving before the sun has risen, injuries, ligaments, high heels, Alexis Kan, rooms you know exist, people you know exist, tree limbs, watermelon, lists, grades, perfume, containers, soup, glasses, countries, oceans, arms, legs, cutting boards, death, TV shows you watched as a child, TV shows you watch as an adult, toilets, factories, exhaustion, depression,

silk, protuberant, insidious, foul language, parental monitoring as the most annoying fucking thing, sweet dusk, boredom, insecticide,

unimportance,

unhappiness, impatience,

BOREDOM,

death, jealousy, desire, (perceptual) perceptional fucktion,

doubtful, hopeless, TIRED,

ungrateful, fleeing, wasted

MY FUCKING WASTED YOUTH, USELESS

You can explain your whole life away and you still won't know who you are.

25 September 2011

Does truth stand the test of time? I am chasing the night in a 747.

28 September 2011

So much has happened. I have not had time to write. After the plane I met with the study abroad people, and we took a bus to the student dorm building, which is huge. It has several floors and is close to King's Cross station. I made friends with two Asian girls, Sakura and Moe, and they are so nice, and don't speak perfect English, but speak very well. Sakura is short and super fashionable, and Moe is taller and really thin. They are yearlong students as well, and my closest friends here. They crack me up. Mostly Sakura. They are both from Osaka, Japan. So tight.

The first day I was tired and hot and cranky. The second day, yesterday, was shitty in the morning because I was having a bit of culture shock and was frustrated and overwhelmed and I couldn't figure everything out and I really wanted to. My internet wouldn't work and my plug adaptor was the wrong type and everything sucked. After enrollment I couldn't find Moe and Sakura and I wanted to change my classes, but when I went to ask the people in charge they said we weren't going over that until later, and I was so frustrated and anxious and I almost started crying and my chin wouldn't stop quivering and I felt SO STUPID. And then I went to the bathroom and cried a little bit because I was so stressed out. After that I wandered around alone.

Once I went to the meeting later everything got way better. I found Moe and Sakura and we explored with this girl named Brynn. She is tiny and funny and looks like Lady Gaga and is from New York. We went to a restaurant and I got a waffle with ice cream for £2, cheap! Two other random study abroad people came too. We rode the tube and got Oyster cards, which is the public transportation card that gets you access to the tube and the buses. This random British guy hit on me and gave me his number, and I'm totally going to call him and make him buy me a drink. He said he was going to get something published, so I'll probs ask him about that as well.

Today we had a meeting about technological stuff, and in about an hour we are doing "fun stuff." I don't know what that means. Slowly I have been figuring my shit out and it's getting way better. I am excited and happy.

30 September 2011

Yesterday we took a boat and bus tour, and it was beautiful. We saw most of the main attractions, and I also made lots of friends! I met an Italian girl who is so nice and fun, and she let me take a hit from her joint, haha. It was a secret! I met some Polish girls who were nice. I took almost a whole roll of fisheye pictures, a couple of Polaroids, and lots of digital pics.

There is a boy named Rob who I can tell is in love with me, but I am not attracted to him at all. Oops. He totally follows me around. There was a party at the student bar last night and it was really fun. There was food and fake tattoos and a bar, and dancing and super loud music. It was great because everyone is nice and friendly and interesting. So many people stare at me, it's awesome. They always say they like my hair, and I feel so genuine.

Today I had a meeting about my modules, and I got all my classes figured out, so I am happy. After that I met Taiki (a boy from Japan), Kara (our tourist tourist guide), Rob (the one in love with me), Yui (cutest Asian girl ever who is very stylish), Blaine (a black guy with green eyes who I think is attractive), and AJ (a girl from Turkey), and we all went exploring. Right now we are hanging out in Green Park, by Buckingham Palace. We visited Piccadilly Circus, where some Italian guys wanted a picture with me, National Gallery and that whole area, and got ice cream in St. James Park. Everything is beautiful and lush, and I have taken many pictures. Right now we are resting in Green Park and the weather is perfect. Breeze, sunny, in the shade. I am where I am supposed to be.

I forgot to say that yesterday this guy from Algeria stopped me on the street before we were going to the bar, and he was in love with me and asked for my number and my Facebook info. I am definitely not attracted to him at all. Good thing I don't have a number.

Today I bought a seven-day rail card for £27.60, so expensive. But worth it, because I can go everywhere in zones one and two as many times as I want. I am going to apply for a student Oyster card when I get back to my room.

01 October 2011

Saturday. Right now I am in Soho Square, the gardens. It's a small park and there are a ton of people sitting on the grass in the shade. The weather here is hot. At least in the sun. I am in the shade right now and it's okay.

I woke up sweating at noon, Moe was being SO LOUD. (Did I mention she ended up being my roommate?) It's okay. Our room is so hot, I hate it. I can't wait for the weather to be cold.

It's the people here that make it good. So many interesting people. So many languages, so many ideas and perspectives. I think I just needed to know they existed. I dunno why.

I'm home now at the student dorm. I'm in the community kitchen eating. I rode a double decker bus for the first time, back to King's Cross. It was hella tight! I need to see everything, all the places that exist.

02 October 2011

I'm sitting in front of St. Paul's fucking Cathedral. I'm going to start crying or something. This is exactly where I'm supposed to be. It's windy and warm. I feel so safe, I feel so safe in London, like everything will be okay because I'm in the right place and I'm supposed to be right here. It's hard to explain. I just have this thing with locations. London is so safe and the transportation system is incredible and I'm getting the hang of it and I can't imagine being anywhere else. The history, the significance, the stories. It means so much.

I need to take it all in, smooth my hands along the stone and architecture. I need to be everything it stands for, feel every person's love for the building as my own love. I have no idea what I'm doing with my life, but I know that for the next eight months I am safe. London will keep me safe. Coming here was the best decision I've ever made.

I'm back in the student dorm kitchen reading *House of Leaves*. I like it so far but I feel like I'm missing a ton of small details.

I went to fucking mass at St. Paul's. They were about to have service when I walked inside (I didn't know you could go in without paying), so I took a leaflet and sat down. It's incredible inside. So much detail and color. Mind blown (once again).

No one will ever be good enough for me.*

Tomorrow is the first day of school. Excite.

[*Ana: Ruler of the 7th conjunct Saturn, sounds about right. –J.]

03 October 2011

I've had my first class, a writing class. It was alright. I talked a little bit and didn't feel like a complete idiot, but I still felt dumb because I hate my American accent. British people just sound so much more intelligent, and they use better words as well. I don't think anyone noticed my discomfort though, so it's fine. I have another class at two, about film history.

These hallways are labyrinthine. Actually, the entire building is a labyrinth, it's quite irritating. Because I can never find the toilet. And I only know a few places to sit and write/read. But I think I could go to the library or something. There are tons of places, I'm sure.

I really enjoy *House of Leaves*. It's so creepy.

I don't really have friends yet, other than Sakura and Moe, but I don't think it will be difficult. People seem to be intrigued by me, so I'll just let whatever happens happen. I want to become friends with old people. I don't know what else.

There are so many possibilities here, it's amazing. I'm not even sure what I'm going to do today. I could probs go somewhere new every day and still not see all the places that exist in the time I will be here.

04 October 2011

I had Film History yesterday and it was long and boring and the seats are uncomfortable. There are long, thin tables that are connected to the seats, and they are too low to write on comfortably. Ugh. After that I was tired and hungry so I ate a shit-ton of food and fell asleep.

Today my alarm didn't go off so I woke up 45 minutes late and was in a rush to class. I wasn't horribly late though, so it was okay. It was a sociology class called Social Problems and a very attractive boy sat behind me but I didn't talk to him. We didn't have seminar after lecture because it's the first week, so I got out early.

Right now I am sitting on a bench in this little park area by the building where my next class is. Microeconomics. There are a ton of business folks here. Lame. I think it's their lunch break. I am trying to find more places to just hang out and read in. I always feel like I need to be going somewhere or doing something, and it makes me anxious. So I want to go to new places, but also sit and read as well. Because I really like my book! Also, today it is perfect. Chilly and overcast. I love being cold as of late. I have been sweating so horribly lately, but it's been okay today.

I have been thinking that I will be single forever. Forever. Because no one is good enough for me ever, like I am just not attracted to anyone. And no one tries to make me their girlfriend, so…whatever. I will probably be a virgin for forever as well. I am too picky.*

[*Ana: You're not too picky, you just have high standards, which is a good thing. Better to be alone than with someone that isn't a good fit. –J.]

I had my microeconomics class, which was forever long, but I understand it easily enough. I think I feel a bit homesick. Well, not really homesick, I just miss my family and my friends. It's going to take a while for me to call this place home. I think it will happen, I just need to give it time. I am eating pesto pasta with mushrooms. I have already eaten a whole jar of Nutella, haha. How horrible.

I think it's hard for me to get used to living without the security of my parents, and so I get nervous and feel weird when I'm on my own. I don't know. I think everyone feels this way sometimes. Oh, I Skyped both Jenna and Tabby! I was supposed to Skype Kan but she never got online because she's dumb. Okay bye.

06 October 2011

Today is Thursday. I got up early and went to the city part of London, like by St. Paul's Cathedral, kind of. I wanted to go to Leadenhall and Smithfield Markets and explore the area around that part of the university campus. I went to Smithfield and it was just super creepy and undergoing construction. I was wearing high heels so I got creepy looks from all the construction workers. So I didn't really shop around there, and I couldn't find the market entrance so I just left.

I found Leadenhall and it was teeny and not really a market, just a few shops and some food stands. But they were like meals, so I didn't get anything. I was expecting fruit or something. So I left and went to the Gherkin, this huge penis-shaped building, haha. I didn't go inside, just walked around it.

Hmm…I had three candy bars for lunch and then took a two or three hour nap, went grocery shopping, and then wandered around the King's

Cross area. I went to Coram's Fields and looked in some shops by this movie theatre called Renoir. It was cool.

Now I'm in the student dorm café. I want to read! Kan and I have another Skype date. My jaws hurt from chewing gum. I wish I had a job. I have that feeling I always had in Seattle about not being a part of anything because I am jobless. I dunno. Even now I feel I have not fully explained that feeling.

Yesterday Sakura and I traveled around the West End. We went to Topshop and Urban Outfitters (where I got a watch and a cute flask to sneak alcohol into clubs/bars/pubs). We also went to Foyle's and a couple other bookstores, and then went to Scoop, this delicious ice cream gelato place. We kept getting lost though, and I was starving and frustrated and in a bad mood, so it sucked for a while.

Sakura is such a slowpoke, and I just want to get shit done and complete missions, but I have to continually wait up for her. For some reason this drives me absolutely insane. Other than her I haven't made any real friends. Moe isn't a real person, and everyone on my floor is super lame and American. Blah blah blah.

I feel like I'm missing out. What a weird thing to feel when I live in fucking LONDON. I'm here, finally! I live here, yet I still don't feel like I belong. I still don't know how to meet people. Like, I see so many people on the street that I want to know, but they are all going somewhere. They all have their own lives and I can't just stop them and say, "Tell me your life story." It just doesn't work like that. That's why I want to get a job, because then it'd be easier to meet people naturally…Fuuuuuck.

I don't know what I am supposed to be doing with my life. I don't know why I need to be doing something. I don't know a lot of things.

07 October 2011

Today I woke at noon and walked to the St. Pancras Gardens. I explored that area, which I think is Camden but I'm not entirely sure. It was pretty sweet. I also explored the British Library, and it will be a neat place to study. There is a café and a ton of places to sit. There were a lot of people but still seats available.

I just finished writing out all the places in London that I want to go to, in lists by area. Exciting. Well, I am going to go read *House of Leaves*. Which I love.

Last night Kan and I Skyped and it was good.

10 October 2011

I have a lot to say and no time at all to say it. I have been struggling. I have to go to class in ten minutes. It's windy and sunny and I'm in the courtyard at the northern campus, but I'm going inside now.

Okay, class is over. We watched a silent film that was so boring I wanted to die. Probably only that boring because I'm used to amazing new technology in the movies. Anyway, I have a meeting with my study abroad program people in an hour. I am in the library right now.

Friday night I went to my first club, called Tiger Tiger. I made out with this guy who was originally from Spain but lives in England and had a British accent. It was fun, but we had to pay 10 pounds to get in. Lame.

Then on Saturday night I got SUPER wasted with Morgan, Brynn, Brynn's friend Amy, and Sakura, and we went to this bar down the street from the student dorm, and it was ridiculous. I made out with two guys that were friends, Toby and Jim, and I guess I was really crazy and ridiculous. I think I was trying to hit on like everyone, haha.

Yesterday Brynn was telling me that I wasn't myself on Saturday night* and, I dunno, kind of lecturing me but not really, and it just really annoyed me. Like, she acted like it was so embarrassing or bad of me to have done all that, and I didn't think it was. I thought it was normal. I don't know. She also acted like I initiated all the making out, and I know I didn't, because Toby totally was initiating most of it. I just felt like she was reprimanding and blaming me. And I was like, who fucking cares? I was drunk, was ridiculous, so what? It doesn't mean anything. She's not my mother; she doesn't even know me for that matter. It's just dumb drama. If I never see those guys again it is perfectly fine with me.

[*Ana: Didn't you have a mental breakdown that night, too? That could be why she said you weren't yourself. She hadn't met your mental breakdown side yet. –J.]

God, I just feel like I'm in Moscow with Camila again, all that fucking pointless drama. So I have been confused today and yesterday and am asking myself questions about life and who I am, and I don't think it's going anywhere. Brynn made it seem like I was rude or offended people, and that made me feel bad because that's definitely not my intention. I just do not understand what is so bad about making out with people. It's fun, it's spur of the moment. I don't have to be faithful to one person. I don't have to love them. Why is everyone so weird?

I guess I just feel embarrassed and bad if someone got upset over my actions. And Brynn just makes me feel so uncomfortable and anxious and like I'm not where I'm supposed to be.

We are all stories in the end.

I cut myself yesterday and I intend on doing it again.

Fuck off, world.

Here are the questions:

1. Was my behavior alienating others?

2. Was my behavior *entirely* my fault? (Toby pressuring me, loss of control when drunk.)

3. Do I overindulge in this sexual behavior because I have been deprived of it and am sexually frustrated?

4. Control or no control? An illusion of control? Do I fear not having control and is that why I feel weird and uncomfortable now?*

5. Can I love others if I don't feel emotionally or mentally attracted to anyone, ever?

6. Do I care about other people? Do I care about their feelings? Can I empathize with them? Or do I only want physicality?

7. If I only want physicality, then what's the point of hanging out with anyone? Because that doesn't start friendships or love or what-fucking-ever.

[*Ana: You fear not having control over your subconscious (is this due to Sun-Saturn-North Node conjunction all in 12th house Capricorn?) so you try to write it away before it can influence you without your consent.** But it will always influence you because you are a part of it. You *must* realize you have little control and learn to let go. Do all you can, yes, but don't worry about the uncontrollable. Learn to float in the silky waters of the Void, content with only Here and Now. –J. Around 21:39, 07 September 2020, Meridian, ID.]

[**J: Is that even true though? Why do you say that? How do you know that? –J. 18:58, 04 April 2023, Boise, ID.]

Suspicions I have about myself:

1. I can't relate to others and this makes me feel unsafe and anxious around them.

2. I need someone that is mentally fucked, more than I am.

3. I think everyone, ESPECIALLY men, has/have ulterior motives. Men only want to fuck you, so I make out with them but don't let them into my mind and my thoughts. Guys and girls can't be friends. Seriously.

4. Dating, going out with a guy, whatever it may be, is so uncomfortable for me, because I feel like the whole reason you do that is to be able to fuck them in the end. So why not just skip the bullshit and get right to

that? I know they aren't listening or are interested in what I have to say, so why pretend? I HATE PRETENDING. I hate the falsity, I hate anything other than the truth. I don't want to play games.

I'm only genuinely interested in you if you are a revolutionary. If you are sincere, if you feel things, if you're sensitive, if you read and write and drink wine and fuck people if you feel like it and do bad things for good reasons and don't give a shit and care so fucking much, and understand that saying what I truly feel is so hard and that I don't even know what I truly feel.

And just let whatever happens, happen. And you wouldn't judge, and you'd be grungy and wear weird outfits but not in a gay, fashionable way, in a Kurt way. And you'd never, ever be dramatic. And you wouldn't be rude or reprimanding, because you know that there is always a reason for human behavior, and that a person isn't a bad person because of an action they take that turns out to be a mistake or to be regretted. And that you can never judge people by what they do or say, because maybe their intentions are different, or maybe they can't decide how they feel or what they want.

Anyway, you don't exist and we'll never find each other.

I know instantly that every man I meet is not you, I see through them all, I can't stand any of them, they're all animals.*

I need intelligence.

[*Ana: Hey, wtf, animals are way better than people lol. –J. 19:03, 04 April 2023, Boise, ID.]

11 October 2011

I feel significantly better. After writing last night I realized that I shouldn't give a fuck what anyone thinks. Also Morgan came to my room to get her alcohol that she left there and said that Brynn has been annoying her lately, and that just made me feel so much better, haha. It made me realize that I'm not on crack and that Brynn is as weird as I thought she was. I mean, I do like her, she's fun, but she doesn't get it. Like the big "IT." Whatever.

13 October 2011

Things I want and HAVE: an infinite array of activities to do, a closet filled with only my favorite things, the weather slightly cold so I can wear layers and dark lipstick and appear sultry and mysterious, friends in London, having people stare at me and admire me, buying my own groceries!

Today is Thursday. I was anxious in the morning because I felt like I was doing everything wrong and money was really worrying me and I don't have a job and I get nervous when I have to talk to people. But then I got groceries at Sainsbury's and I felt so much better. And I found a Barclay's ATM and got £200 out, which is how much money I can spend a month.

I also got my reader pass at the British Library and finished my reading for Film History. I got a caramel mocha from Costa, and they seriously have the best caramel mochas EVER. I had been craving one and I kind of had a headache, so after I got it I felt so much better. I just feel better about life now.

Yesterday I did some errands at north campus, and then Sakura and I explored the area around the other campus – close to Shoreditch and Spitalfields, and I LOVE it. Everyone is eclectic and cool and I got the best vibes ever. We are going to explore that area more. It fucking blew my mind, and I think I found a cool place to develop my film. I might ask them what I should do about my broken fisheye flash. I fit in, I belong, in Shoreditch, Spitalfields, blah, blah, blah. I adore it.

I love how Sakura and I are so alike. We like a ton of the same things: art, fashion, books. It's the best ever. She is sociable and people instantly like her, so that will help me meet people as well.

Tonight I rearranged my desk and it is great now. Oh, I forgot to say that Sakura and I want to get seahorse tattoos! I'm totally going to, I will force her to as well. I feel organized since I cleaned my desk and got groceries and did my homework. Now I am going to do my Econ homework. I love you.

14 October 2011

Today was good. I returned books to the library, figured out how to send mail to the US, and also explored a bit around Angel, Aldgate, and White Chapel tube stations. It was sunny today so I took my fisheye and photographed a lot of architecture and stuff that needed light to look good.

It's Friday and I do not know if I'm doing anything tonight. I feel like I'm not because I dunno what other people are doing. I hate all the Americans on my floor, they are seriously so annoying. Maybe I will see what Sakura is doing, she is my best friend here! I love it. Well, I guess that is all, I can't think of what else.

15 October 2011

Today I explored the South Bank. I saw Shakespeare's Globe Theatre and walked across the London Bridge and Millennium Bridge. I wore an awesome outfit and everyone looked at me and I looked fucking fabulous. I also finished my reading for my writing class and wrote Grandma a letter. Oh, I also went to Borough Market and it was so great! Tons of food, veg, fruit, meat, everything.

Last night Sakura and I ended up going to Club 333 in Shoreditch with the ridiculous Americans from my floor. And it was okay. I am reinforced of my low opinion and expectations of clubs, though. I feel like they mostly consist of a ton of people crowded together. Lame. And you can't talk to people because the music is way too loud.

Sakura and I found our way back home with this guy on my floor named Travis. Him and I had a snack in our kitchen and then totally made out. It was so funny and awesome! He is funny and pretends to be awkward but isn't for real. I dunno. I'm not especially attracted to him but I liked kissing him. I kind of want to make it a goal to make out with someone every time I am drunk. Because it's fucking fun and it's free love. And I think guys here just might find me attractive, I have NO idea why.

I totally forgot to say that on the tube today I made eye contact with this guy and looked away, and then looked back, and then he wouldn't stop looking at me, and I would smile and look away and like lick my lips kind of, and he totally wanted me, you could tell. It was the best thing ever. A thrill kind of, because no guy has ever been that bold that wasn't hella creepy and/or of a different ethnicity than me, which I'm not really attracted to. He just kept making eye contact and smiling, and I would smile like I knew something he didn't. And then when I got off the tube he was looking at me and I glanced back and smiled and I felt SO COOL and like a REAL PERSON! So amazing. I want more things like that to happen. It felt like the movies.

Tonight I think we are going to bar hop or some shit. I don't even know. I am hungry and am going to make dinner soon.

17 October 2011

OMFuckingG. When we went to the bar on Saturday we went to Be @ 1, and I ran into this French Algerian guy like twice, and I ended up sleeping over at his friend's house with him on the futon. Ha. We didn't have sex though, which is good.

In the morning he made this huge delicious breakfast and it was great. And they talked in French with an Arabic twist the whole time. So cool to listen to. I dunno if I will see them again because I don't have a phone, but he has Brynn's number. I guess he texted her four times yesterday. Which is weird and clingy. He kind of had gross legs, but whatever. I liked his face. They smoked cigarettes inside. And we rode in a black cab to get to his friend's house, as well as one of those bicycle things where the people on the bikes pull you around in a tiny carriage. Haha. Funny.

Today is Monday and classes were okay. Film History felt much shorter than usual, so that was nice. I felt like I was going to fall asleep in my writing class. I blogged Kan today and it was the longest thing ever, but it felt really good, cathartic. I miss her and I feel like we haven't talked in forever. Same with Zara.

Mentioning Zara reminds me that I bought tickets for a White Lies concert here! I got the tickets today. So excited. Tomorrow I have classes and then the study abroad theatre trip to see *Wizard of Oz*. Should be interesting. I want to wear something awesome and fabulous.

I love this teeny diary. I feel accomplished when I don't spend money. I want to meet more people and have intellectual conversations. Well, I guess that is all, I dunno.

18 October 2011

15 minutes until my class Social Problems starts. I think I like my outfit. I am not wearing a bra. I love it here, it's how things are supposed to be. It's hard to explain. Like how efficient the transportation system is, and the multitude of pubs and bars and clubs, and I dunno. I adore it. I can't get over how many opportunities there are here, and I'm so fucking jealous of the people that were born here.

What I want to do with my life:

–publish book

–finish college

–grad school somewhere awesome

20 October 2011

Today is Thursday. I went to Regent's Park and Daunt Books this morning and then went grocery shopping. And Skyped Sakura. And took a nap. Now I'm in the café at the dorm pretending to do homework.

Last night I went with the people on my floor to a place called The Roadhouse. It's a club, and it was fun, I guess, but I didn't make out with anyone! So ends my streak. But I will try to make a new streak. Sakura lost her purse last night on the tube so she didn't end up going with us.

Yesterday I worked out in the morning but then I felt sick. Like, I felt like throwing up would be a good idea, so I just slept for around four hours, and then it was dark out. Lame. So I wasted the day kind of. Well, whatever.

I decided I am in love with Taiki because he is from Japan and fucking hilarious and I feel like he is in love with me too. Haha.

Oh, the *Wizard of Oz* play! It was really good, way better than I expected. The set was fucking insane and high tech. I took a couple pics and got in trouble for it, haha. We got there right when it started so we sat in the back kind of, but you could still see perfectly.

I feel like I don't like anything. Like, I do things, like go to the play or visit places in London, and it's fun, but I dunno. I feel like I want to go to places and do different things just so I can say that I did it. Because the actual activity is, like, whatever. It's cool, but it's never *that* big of a deal, or *that* fucking amazing. I dunno, it's weird in my mind.

21 October 2011

Today is Friday but I am tired so I don't think I'm going to go out. I am also starving so I'm going to make some pasta.

Last night we went to the Big Chill House in Shoreditch and there were so many interesting people! Sakura and I walked by that exact bar when we explored that area the other week. So cool. Taiki bought me a drink and I ended up sleeping in his bed, which was fucking tiny and uncomfortable. We sort of hooked up but not really. He asked me to give him a blowjob and I laughed really hard and said no. Haha. He is a horrible kisser. I feel like our hook up session lasted 45 seconds. Seriously.

Then today I showered and took a long nap and then explored more of the South Bank. I went to a movie at the BFI for the London Film Festival. It was called *Shock Head Soul* and it was boring as fuck. I didn't like it at all. I thought it was going to be super interesting because it was about insanity and stuff, but it wasn't. It was slow and LAME.

24 October 2011

Lots of things have happened. First of all, yesterday I went on a day trip to Stonehenge, Bath, and Windsor with Monica, a girl who lives on my floor. She is nice. I'm really glad I got to have that experience. I took so many pictures! I think my fisheye is fucked up now though, because I tried to load a new roll of film and it wouldn't go. God.

On Saturday Sakura and I explored Brick Lane, so cool! I definitely want to go back because at the market there was a sweet shirt with Kurt Cobain on the front! I want to buy it I think. I feel bad because Sakura drives me absolutely insane sometimes and I find it hard to pay attention to her. So I tune out on accident while she's talking. Oops. She is just so scatterbrained and she takes FOREVER to look around shops, and to say what she wants to say, and to complete simple tasks. And she always wants to look at the map even when I'm 100% sure of where we're going. So goddamn annoying, haha. I mean, I still think she's awesome and my best friend here, just ridiculous as well.

I wonder if it's a cultural thing though, because Moe is also really ridiculous sometimes, too. The Irks & Quirks of Moe: So fucking loud when she has to get ready and I don't, as well as when I go to bed before her (slams door, rustles bags and papers, etc.); asks me what I'm eating for dinner when it's clearly in front of me for her to see; asked me what tube stop she could get off at to see Stonehenge; doesn't ask me about my day, my life, what my opinion is of anything (in fact, I doubt she cares about me at all…).

Anyway, it's alright, because she is easy to live with and not clingy or talkative or whatever.

I've been wanting to say a lot of things. First, I miss psychology. I'm not taking any psychology classes right now and I hate it because it's the only thing that interests me, and it always helps me figure my shit out, and makes me feel studious and intellectual. And I like *want* to do psych homework. Ugh. I don't want to do the readings I have to do for my current classes. I want to study at coffee shops because I haven't been doing that!

Personal liberation, Anemic Cinema, Nihilism, Anarchic

I need this journal. I need my own words breathless and sparked and nonsensical and hurtful and published and worrisome and anxious and the death urges. My anemic emotional handwriting that may not be my own, alone. No right, no wrong, too much caffeine and not enough water. Notebooks, lyrics, flimsy paper, fighting, commas, cafés, languages erupting from our tongues, we use our mouths. You are eclectic in your sweater and knits and patterns and dirt. You are dirty you are my everything I do not love you I cannot love anything.

The weeks flying by, on your wings, your time, your clockwork. I wonder if you are the clockmaker. I remember certain vibes, an atmosphere made of dark silk, menacing mind waves and ugly paintings and things I want to say. Emphasis on expressionism, that's all it may be, it may be a mix of things that only add up to the color brown. Beige confusion, milky coffee, spontaneous chance music happenings, words I'll never say.

Intoxication, bubbling happiness released from neurons, endorphins, a bottle of happiness with a message from the sand, the seaweed. Notes of importance, plans, thoughts, ideal worlds of shittiness, popularity, the girls of yesterday, my dreams in fleeting underwater images, your bottled message floating away unread, my catharsis somehow wrong if anything could be wrong.

My bad choices leading to dulled pencils and no sharpener. On and on, and on forever, and we'll still never interpret correctly. It's not beautiful, it's probably meaningless sadness mixed with longing and regret and distrustfulness and made up words and no words, just fragments of lost pictures, of too much ice cream and far too few moments in this life. Of dissatisfaction and the tone of your voice.

25 October 2011

The ultimate question I freak out about is: Is anything better than anything else?

My "things": locations, religions, types of people, fame and lack of fame, to be alone or with others.

Things I want: to run far and fast, to see every part of London, to get all my homework done in a coffee shop that isn't packed but has a good view, to wear all of my clothes equally much, and I'm wondering if I need to get rid of even more clothes if I want that to happen…

26 October 2011

Big Chill Bar in Shoreditch with a hot chocolate and Microecon homework. Sakura is next door at the music store getting a tutorial or something concerning her classes. Not really sure. Bars are weird, I dunno. I feel weird writing in here. I feel like it's a weird thing to do. Oh well, it's a fucking Wednesday, people. It's 4:35 p.m.

Today I have been getting shit done, it's good. I feel okay. I'm annoyed now because I paid £1.70 for the smallest hot chocolate in the entire world, and I don't understand my Microecon homework. God. And I didn't go to the British Library and I needed to. I think I'm gonna go back to the dorms and do my laundry and eat a fuckin' donut. Fuck.

Also, I'm not sure if I'm supposed to leave my dishes here at the table or bring them to the counter. And this makes me so anxious. Isn't that weird that that makes me uncomfortable? It makes me crazy.

27 October 2011

I'm in a park in the West End. Actually, it's more like a garden, sheltered under a tree from the rain, sitting on a bench. It's my favorite weather: the sky is white-grey but bright, and it's cold enough for my leather jacket but not so cold that I can't sit outside and write this. I needed some alone time, but outside, not in my dorm.

I like my outfit today because I'm wearing clothes I haven't worn in what feels like forever. Brown tights, thick socks, hiking boots, leather jacket. These things need love.

I try to systematically categorize my thoughts and I shouldn't because it's kind of impossible. How does my mind smooth over today's emotional vibrations? I need water, I need time, I need past histories not my own, I need you but I don't want to and I don't think I do. I need art to spur on my will to live. I imagine my mind as a valley of hills and crevasses and meadows. Ridges and folds lost in a white mist, secret caves left for dead.

I'm an explorer mapping the area between lines of black, eraser marks failing to keep up with the changes. The valley changes like the corridors and walls and ceiling and floor of Navidson's house. The changes are subtle and I am tiny. I'll never say it all. Will you perceive it as a work of art?

I want paper, I want assignments and logic and intelligence. I want to write something important. I want meaning and purpose and money as a side effect. I don't want rules, I want a creative balance between right and wrong. I want relationships with people that are sad and hate everything.* I want to be more important than the rest. I want to be sloppy and still look good, like Miss Courtney Love and her dream boy Kurt. I don't want any more jewelry or things.

[*Ana: Maybe you'll always get what you want. Only Time will tell. –J.]

Pupils as pinpricks boring into the souls of the buildings, cutting through brick the way I cut into my own heart, dismembering my own soul and desire, leaving me nameless and faceless and drenched in an apathy labeled as indifference. An abstraction I'll never understand, an abstraction I want another to explain to my face.* I don't want just anyone. I fear insignificance. My mind is devoured by fear and longing.

[*Ana: You want to be *the* 12th house case study. You want to be a thorough and enduring example of how astrology works. You're the abstract Aquarian with Venus in the first house, haunted by Saturn's gravitational pull on your subconscious. Well, here we are, still waiting for an astrologer educated in history and mythology to show us our many faces. We will pull him in closer, a spider waiting for the fly, darkness as sexual and inviting, eyes revealing predatory instincts, using Time as a weapon. We'll wait for you forever because you are the only one. –J. around 11:27 a.m. on 11 September 2020. Meridian, ID]

Fucking Hell

I'm full I'm too full why aren't the lines corresponding to my writing? I'm going to get fucking drunk tonight and forget about my worries (which are: money, being able to get a job, being able to love or be loved).

28 October 2011

THINGS: walking for hours under a hooded sky, upon damp cobblestones, learning, adapting, doubt, nervousness, always finding something to worry about, beautiful histories not my own, desire, satisfaction, wandering, appearances as deceptive, memories, the future as impossible to perceive, snacking, heartburn, the smell of rot, reading, burnt out light bulbs, images igniting creativity, hopelessness, fear, locked doors, wanting to know everyone on a personal level, waiting for miracles that never come, over exaggeration, looking good,

hating everyone, not finding the words, not feeling secure, wanting a job because that may bring a sense of security, colors fading, too much jewelry, too many material items, not utilizing one's resources, like the paints and paintbrushes available, not knowing what I want, not knowing what sounds enjoyable, not finding anyone of interest, feeling bloated, Kurt wearing a dress as the sexiest thing I have ever seen, wanting to be a part of something badly but never having it happen, lists, Polaroids, growing out one's hair, trying to create something interesting,

European police sirens, Oreos, arrows, looking for art, finding it in bookstores and desiring it and disliking that desire and wanting to make your own damn art, weheartit.com, words that inspire, the colours of your soul, British nuances, living in London, going somewhere new every day, Costa Coffee as a safe place, strange currency, instability, crying, you, attractive boys with fashionable clothes, plans, being sick, watching people stare at you while riding the underground, wanting to use up all the things I own so I can get rid of them and not have any more things,

immortality, wanting to publish a book, wanting to do a whole bunch of things but not knowing how to get involved, wanting a motherfucking boyfriend so life would be interesting, relief upon finding a good vibe, a healthy choice, an incredibly unhealthy choice, postcards, being asked where you're from, pictures, cameras, organizing, food, coffee, alcohol, need, pencil cases, boxes, backpacks, transcribing, buses, mugs, staying up late, sleeping in,

two days of class and five days of weekend, freedom, trapped in an anxiety cage, concerts, maps, disinterest, fashion, love as a fallacy, headaches, disbelief at my forgetfulness, misplacing needed items, DIY, stealing sugar packets, Skype, one real friend everywhere I go, hanging out in my room on my Macbook, paper, blood vessels close to the top layer of skin and how ugly that looks, painting, recycling, being a bad cook, communicating,

Undated

rain, heart, darkness but it's not late, eye contact, the reflection of lights in the windows, umbrellas, wet hair, the lives of strangers, this is where I'm meant to be, accents everywhere, time zones, dilated pupils, people being similar around the globe, "other people's lives are such mysteries," shitty cursive handwriting as quirky and perhaps creative, planning what to pack on trips, colours, intellectual endeavors, wanting more homework and wondering if that's a strange thing to desire,

the blending of various mediums in order to create something revolutionary, hunger?, waiting, doodles, bad quality, almost having the hair of your dreams, mental instability, avoiding people that like you, wanting to be in love with someone but no one is loveable, smoking cigarettes, luck, circumstance, not being bothered by text messages, wanting to try beans on toast, words, words, the appearance of languages not understood,

WRECKAGE

defeat!

29 (?) October 2011

I'm in the Bunhill Fields Burial Ground, it's 4:10 p.m. and silent. It's visibly autumn. The leaves are light brown and yellow, strewn all over the ground. Crows, squirrels. The light is bright but hidden behind trees and passing clouds. A cold breeze rustles the trees and the leaves that haven't fallen yet. There is a man photographing the graves.

This is harmony at the center of technological chaos. This is a haven for the departed, for my lost soul, for wanderers and the unsure.

I finished *House of Leaves* this morning. I liked it. Now I'm going to read a short novel called *City of Thieves*.

Last night Sakura and I went to this art exhibition slash house party, and it was really interesting. We didn't even get drunk, we just watched these documentary things. I feel better about my uncertainty about the future because of those videos. They told stories about real people who were in the same boat as me, kind of, or worse off and still making it. So I guess I felt hopeful, even though that word/concept is super lame.

I also went grocery shopping, and returned my old Oyster card, which I got £5.50 back for. Tite. I learned that Sainsbury's is infinitely better than Tesco. Cool. Well, that's all for now. The light is failing. I'm going to try to find a coffee shop to study in…

FINALLY! I found a motherfucking Costa, in Angel. And it's beautiful. My chair is cushy and I'm sitting at a table. I got a gingerbread latte and I'm eating one of the chocolate chip muffins I got last night after the art exhibit. I am so comfortable. And it doesn't close until eight p.m.

If I lived alone and had my own job and bought my own groceries and supplies, I would probably buy cheap sweets and go to a lot of coffee shops. It's so weird how I do that here, like go to McDonald's and buy pastries and shit, when I would never do that if I lived at home with my parents. I think it depends on where you live, and who you live with. I dunno.

I am trying to study right now. And I'm really excited about it, haha. I like my outfit and I want to wear it more often. I'm wearing the shirt I have that says "talk to me," a dark green corduroy skirt, and black fishnet tights from Hot Topic. And Hello Kitty shoes. Boo fucking yah.

30 October 2011

Collections, collage, art galleries, houses alone in the countryside (cottages), drawing, never looking back, VIBES.

I feel a lot better about life lately. Mainly because I have started being more creative because I found my sketchbook and I've been looking through my past hearts on weheartit.com. It feels so good. I feel like things will be okay.

I also emailed the student dorm residence manager about applying for a position as a resident assistant, because they get motherfucking paid, and I feel like I'd be able to do it with ease. I dunno, I just really want it to work more than anything. Now I wonder if you have to have been here for more than just a semester in order to apply. Fuck. Oh well, whatever happens, happens.

Undated

a line of sweat
a sliver of shade
watery light, a hardbound book
broken jewelry
a dying motion
blood all over the walls

uniform structures, indivisible objects

an eternal breath in

imperceptible threads
the vibration of your sound waves
a void never filled
my brain high on abstractions

an infinite cosmos
an unanswerable question
a worthless goal
a self-fulfilling prophecy

a wasted, futile thought

a revolution never formed

your hands clasped
a mind divided, a consciousness warped
a model of the earth

fear of a disease, of no escape
unlimited, open-ended darkness
reason tightened into a fact

a freezing illusion,
particles contradicting
violently persuasive concepts

desire as unreliable

consuming sound, digesting thought, shitting ideas

31 October 2011

Wherever I go I find something to be anxious about. Here it's money. Home it was my body and calories, because there wasn't anything else to worry about. Seattle was both plus Chadwick, which was hell. I just think it's interesting that my anxiety always finds a way to peek through.

I am a tad bit nervous about my weight, but not nearly as much as I have been before. Mom sent me a reassuring email about money, saying that I don't have to worry, and it made me feel a lot better.

Last night Sakura and I went to the South Bank to see a movie at the Mediatheque, and the one we were going to see totally was not at the Mediatheque. It was like a normal movie. So we didn't get to see it. Fucking lame. So we walked around and looked in shops and stuff. I got those little graph paper Moleskin notebooks I've been wanting, I'm excited.

–know people are different but don't know how, in what way, to what extent

Right now I am on a 30-minute break in Film History. Thank god. I always sit by Blaine and JR, because I know them from the dorms, but I decided today that I don't like them. Like, they don't even talk to me at all. Blaine completely turns his body away from me and just talks to JR. And for some reason this annoys the shit out of me.

I guess JR is going to be Fred Flintstone for Halloween, and when I asked him (purely out of curiosity!) if British people know what that is – the show – he was like, "I don't care, *I* know what it is," in this rude tone, and it seemed like he thought I was insulting him because he sounded really defensive about it. He did that thing Americans do where they completely disregard what you say, or like wave it off and ignore you. And that just made me hate him. And hate Sakura for having a crush on him and not being able to see that he is stupid and rude (only because English is her second language, it's really not her fault). It made me hate all the stupid, fucking close-minded and uninteresting Americans on my floor. So irritating. So I decided that I'm not going to sit with Blaine and JR anymore.

This morning in my writing class I talked to this British girl that sits by me named Jessica, for the longest time, all about the differences between here and America.* It was so interesting! I enjoyed it, even though our class was three hours long instead of two. I realized that her life is so fucking different than mine, but not necessarily better. Like, she doesn't know what she wants to do either, and she seemed like she didn't think it was a big deal. It made me feel okay. And safe.

Because it really isn't a big deal; life will work itself out in the end. I dunno. Talking to her made me realize that I am better off than so many people in the world, but not in a guilty way. Living in America really does have benefits. More choices, more opportunities. I think I like that. I dunno, it's complicated. Okay, that is all, I suppose.

[*Ana: It's annoying to me that you keep referring to the US as "America." There are other "Americas"! You're forgetting Central and South America, plus North America includes Canada as well as Greenland, and when you refer to the States as "America" it makes me feel weird because it feels imperialistic, like the US claims itself as the most important place in the Americas. I kind of want to edit you so that you only refer to the US as the US or as the States, but I won't. –J.]

I am pissed because the department chair of psychology at BSU emailed me back about my credits transferring from Seattle and basically said that I can't take any of the psych classes I want/need to take. I seriously hate her, because she acts like I am a fucking idiot and it's so annoying. Like, I wanted to take Cognitive Psych because she said before that my credits from my Learning and Cognition class from Seattle would not be equivalent to Cognitive Psych, and then now in her email she was like, "You already have a Cognitive Psych credit." What the fuck lady, make up your fucking mind! She said I can't take Research Methods but I know I can because I took Stats over the summer and that is the prerequisite.

So I'm angry and frustrated about this. I'm tired because it's late and I know I have to get up at 7:15 a.m. I am nervous about upcoming essays and not wanting to write them. I want attention from guys but I don't like anyone and it's so boring not liking anyone. Travis likes me, it is so fucking obvious, and I am not attracted to him because he is not in shape, but I've already made out with him twice when drunk so he thinks I like him. Fuck. So those are all the things I have been feeling today.

SO. DUMB.

Unconscious art, art without knowing, human beings as works of art, real people that do things simply because what they want to do sounds enjoyable. "I think I'll buy this fucking candy bar because I really am craving it." Admiration from others and suspecting they admire but never knowing for sure. Boredom, entrapment, wanting yet not wanting, dualism, contradictions, lies, writing, paper, folders, small containers for secrets, seeing oneself as palpable, versatile, complex, eager, knowledgeable, thoughtful, imaginative, free, not bothered by petty things, knowing it's alright.

All these things must be true if they were not true they'd be lies I'm horribly lying I'm a liar I'm a fucker I'm a cutter I'm a thinker not a speaker but I have a lot to say, which is always lost in the currents, the vibrations, the pavements of forgotten years, moments, tears, good things wonderful things yet black and coated in tar and blood and caged in a tiny desert house with no water or air, only doubt separated by commas and drives to the store and lathered with love that is deserved but never feels deserved, for no reason,

but I try to escape it, the spread of it, caked like thick butter on a bread knife, this act, of attempted escape, is fat on calories of guilt and regret and anxiety

anxiety
anxiety

YET poetic I should be grateful should I be?

Is there a right way to form words and sounds, a "correctness" of speech, of vowels and lines? Am I doing it wrong, who is to say? Who is to judge the meaning of my scrambled eggs?

My imprecise pinpoint of thought…

my twisted fucker love

I want to be obliterated.

01 November 2011

Last night a ton of people went to this party called Fuck Me It's Halloween. You had to pay £7 to get in, and people were trying to get me to go but I didn't want to pay and I didn't really feel like it, and then just now these two American guys on my floor told me that they didn't end up going because it was like a mosh pit and horrible. So they paid for tickets and didn't go. HA HA HA sucks to be them! I'm so glad I didn't go now! So yeah.

I have to go to Econ in 40 minutes, I don't want to. Then I guess I'm doing this Jack the Ripper tour after, but I dunno if I want to that badly because it's right after class and I'll be drained. Oh well, I can always leave in the middle, I guess. It's free, so whatever.

02 November 2011

I ended up not going to the tour; I just didn't really feel like it. I went to this job fair at the university just now, but it was super lame so I left. It's hot in here.

I am now in the dorm lounge. I need to start writing my essay and I don't want to. I worked out this morning because I feel fat. I also bought some groceries. I wanted to go to a coffee shop but I never did. But it's okay because I'm really tired and I think I might do that tomorrow. Ugh, there is nothing else.

03 November 2011

Overcast, coffee, good vibes emanating from an outfit never worn before, no hunger, wind in trees but other than that silence, alone, calm, timeless atmosphere.

Last night I Skyped my parents for the first time, it was really cool. I also started my essay for my writing class and I think it's alright. I couldn't sleep so I watched *500 Days of Summer*, and it made me feel good, less anxious, I dunno. Hopefully today I will find a coffee shop to study in.

I also need to go to school to read some articles online for my essay. For some reason they don't show up on my laptop, so hopefully they will in the library at the university.

I think there are more things to be said, but I'm not sure what. Well, whatever.

05 November 2011

Today is Guy Fawkes Day. I am going to see fireworks and eat pizza, organized by my study abroad program. Cool.

Yesterday I went to this Japan meeting thing with Sakura and it was fun. We met a ton of Japanese people and played games and then went out to eat at this kebab place by north campus. It was so fun listening to them talk to each other in Japanese.

But Sakura said I was fat. Like, at dinner. And it really hurt my feelings. She said my stomach was just a little bit fat, and I seriously do not understand. Like: 1. Why would she say that? (Because you don't say stuff like that to people, even if it's true.) 2. My stomach isn't, like, abnormally fat. I've always hated it but it's not like I have a giant potbelly or anything, so I don't get it. 3. It's fucking with my mind because how do you even define "fat"? What is that? And people have said I have a nice stomach, like Josh and Camila when I was in Moscow, so I don't get it.

But Sakura is fucking tiny so I guess I would be fat compared to her. I dunno. It just sucks because I've always been super insecure about my body, so it's hard for me to just forget about small comments like this. It also doesn't even matter! Seriously. Guys still think I'm attractive, I am able to work out and do things without being hindered by my weight (like Tabby), and yeah, I dunno. I just overanalyze shit because that's what I do (it's why I'm a Psych major) and it's just stupid. So yeah.

I kind of couldn't stop thinking about why she said this, and it ruined the rest of my night. Oh well, my existence is tiny and insignificant and pointless, who fucking cares if my stomach does not align with Sakura's perfection views?

Anyway, guess who's not a virgin anymore?? This girl! (Me). Hahaha! On Thursday some stupid Americans from my floor and I went to the Rocket Bar down the road (where good things will probably always happen) and I met these three British guys, Jack, Paul, and Michael. Michael asked me if I liked Jack and I said I did. So we all smoked cigarettes outside and talked. Then after multiple long make-out sessions I went home with Jack (Paul and Michael came over later because Paul lives there as well and Michael spent the night) and we totally fucked.

It hurt at first but then it was okay. Actually, it was kind of boring. Like, he enjoyed it but I was like okay, I'm done, this is not actually pleasurable in reality. I refused to give him a hand or blowjob, haha. Because dicks gross me out so badly, and I would have no idea what I'm doing anyway. He didn't believe that I'd never had sex, because I'm that good. Just kidding, I dunno if I'm good. Probably not because I didn't really do anything other than lay there and try to flex my kegel muscles. I don't really know what to do or how to do it correctly. I wore my over-the-knee socks in bed though and he liked that a lot. Weird.

In the morning we had tea and crumpets and it was so delicious. He toasted them and put butter on them, so good. Then he walked me to the tube station and I left. And he added me on Facebook.

I am pleased with myself because I wasn't wasted when it happened and he was not a creeper and it happened with a British guy in London. And now I'm not sexually frustrated anymore!* Now I just don't even care to have sex because it wasn't even that exciting and I'll know what I'm missing when I say no. It's not much. So…yeah. I suppose that's all for now.

[*Ana: Yeah, you are. You didn't even come.

The astrology of that night is super interesting. It would be 03 November 2011 – the Thursday before you wrote this entry – but late at night and maybe it was even after midnight, so it could have been early morning on the 4th. That night the Moon in late degrees Aquarius was conjunct Neptune at 28° Aquarius as well as Chiron at 00° Pisces, all tightly opposing Mars at 26° Leo, and all four of those were pretty tightly squaring your natal Mars at 28° Taurus. Then, Mercury and Venus, who both rule you this year according to annual profections, were conjunct in the first couple degrees of Sag, so opposing your natal Mars and squaring the Moon-Neptune-Chiron-Mars action. The Sun in Scorpio was squaring your Venus-Jupiter opposition, too.

It's interesting because as you're in an 8th/9th house profection year (profecting from the 12th and 1st houses), one manifestation of that could be losing your virginity in a foreign country. Sex belonging to the 8th house and foreign countries belonging to the 9th house. You've got Virgo in the 8th and Libra in the 9th, and Mercury (ruler of Virgo) was conjunct Venus (ruler of Libra), both opposing your natal Mars, which has much to do with sex.

The Moon-Neptune-Chiron conjunction all opposite Mars is super interesting. The conjunction was in your first house (except Chiron), so representing you, and Mars in the 7th, representing him. You didn't really know how you felt about it (Moon-Neptune) but you didn't like it (Chiron); it wasn't pleasurable or empowering or even a little interesting, and you kinda just did it so that you could not be a virgin anymore, not because you were actually into that guy, who you never saw again. It didn't make you feel particularly good about yourself. You felt just a vague, anticlimactic relief that you didn't have to keep being a virgin.

That's all I'm gonna say about this at this point in time because that's all that really stands out to me right now with my current knowledge of astrology. I'm 100% sure that there's a lot more about how this is hitting Ana's chart that I'm totally missing because of a lack of knowledge. –J.]

07 November 2011

Admirable people and why:

–Damon Albarn: strange romance, bleak, post-apocalyptic world of grayness, mystery, feeling, no rules for how to feel or behave, weird as good/genuine

–Björk: exotic, imagination, creation, destruction, animal, instinctual, roaring intuition, violently passionate

–Kurt: thought his art was shitty, sensitive, angry, messy, said whatever he wanted, protective, poetic, funny, dirty, important, grew up poor in the middle of nowhere

–Courtney: fucking bold, angry, messy, animate, real

Ten minutes until my writing class. I left the dorms a bit early so I could pick up the study abroad theatre ticket and get a tea. Blah blah.

Guy Fawkes Night was so legit. We went to Pizza Express, which is fucking tasty, and then watched fireworks. Right over our heads, with music. So cool. And then later I got hella drunk and went to a couple bars with Amy, a random girl named Victoria, Moe, and Sakura, and it was alright. Then Sakura and I hung out with Travis and slept on the dorm lounge couches. Ha, so great.

Today was good too, because I was productive. Kinda. I stole a ton of sugar packets, I worked out, I got groceries, I worked on my essay. All good things. It's midnight and I'm not sure if I am actually tired, but I'm going to go to bed anyway. I also Skyped Kan a bit today as well, which was nice. I started my period today.

I think that I want to fuck Travis when my period ends. I want to be violent with him, but I think I'll need to get drunk first. Hmm. Yeah, I want to get drunk in order to practice sex, so that I won't be afraid to try the same stuff when I'm sober. Hahaha I am totally crazy! Okay well that is all, I guess.

I have to wake at seven a.m. GROSS!

Undated

This pen is permanent, black, pungent, ready to bleed, saturated, new.

I am impermanent, white, clean and fresh, dry, old. I might be ready to bleed through.

All over the shoes, the floor, the walls, the sink, the bathtub, the perfect pages of this smooth book, your hands, your heart, your love. I'm going to rip out your heart and throw it away. I'm going to give you all my toxins, my thoughts, my impulses. I'm going to hurt you. I'm going to fuck you, I'm going to lie to you. I'm going to ignore you. And then I'm going to leave you, dispose of you.

I will find some new experiment to trash.

I will never love you.

Will you cling to me anyway?

10 November 2011

Good vibrations: black-tipped nails, sweatshirts over dresses, almost finishing a book and starting another, secret uninhabited parts of London that aren't touristy, cloudy gray mornings with coffee and thick socks and braided hair and alone, wearing the same clothes over again, letting the laundry pile up, silence, Polaroids, art museums, opportunity, the smell of autumn darkness, of crunchy leaves, of colorful leaves, of leaves falling, the moon, the fucking white lunar brilliance of some strange orb I wish I could be,

the unity creativity breeds, stupid art, double decker buses, wanting to be cold, waking up sweating, comfortable desk chairs, memories, never getting the coffee/milk ratio right and being pissed about it, packing, planning what to pack, not drinking enough water, photography as a strange medium to channel one's energy, getting rid of all my things, no more things, I don't want to buy anything ever again, hot liquids, making things for other people, trying not to be worried and anxious, not washing my hair, long hair, long nails, texture, wondering how many times I've repeated myself, sex, sex as boring and unintellectual, wanting to want someone, wanting to know everything in someone's mind, needing that fuel, needing another voice, another opinion, reflections in water, pills for depression, thinking I'm fat, the lines on notebook paper, the perforated lines ready to be torn, feathers, obsessions, bananas, not wanting anyone, just wanting to see people admire me, afternoon sunlight appearing through a break in the clouds, inspiration coming from small instances,

washing my face, not knowing the time by looking at the weather, hunger, photographs of family, other people's drawings, fire, cigarettes, auras, your aura mixed with mine and what may be produced, not being satisfied, not thinking something is right because it's not perfect, it must feel perfect, it must feel like it's supposed to happen, curtains on windows, boat houses on canals, flower pots, slight humidity, pebbles, me lost in the crinkled pages of time, growing out my bangs, the fading colors of your hair, freckles and moles, home as wherever you sleep at night,

eyelashes, pajamas until two p.m., staying up late, touching the stone of old buildings and feeling history under your fingers, scraped against your palms the stories of thousands, shiny nail polish, writing but never quite defining, feeling pointless and indecisive, one night stands?, only feeling attracted to people when intoxicated, the darkness comes early, I never come, London, London? Really? Am I in London?, feeling the impact, my favorite music, BBC Live Lounge with Gorillaz making me love Damon Albarn more than I love myself,

statements that may be true or false, nobody knows, turning the pages into the future, baby powder, cheap food, perfume, letters and postcards, other people's rooms, an unclogged shower drain as the safest thing, questions about science, the internet as dangerous yet fascinating, trying to not sound American, liking America more now that I've seen what it's like not being there, catharsis as a really great word, other people's teeth, my teeth as being nice, you know, white, straight, the English language is absurd, bacchanal, nimbus, lives remembered from books I've read, being pleased with a particular outcome, almost missing soccer, that feeling when you score, that feeling when you know you're fucking good at soccer, running, release, page numbers, writing essays, psychology as my favorite thing, thinking that perhaps I'm intelligent, wanting to write a book, not knowing how to get involved,

11 November 2011

At a Costa who knows where. Westminster, I think. I just walked down Fleet Street. I smoked two cigarettes. I'm mad because my coffee tastes like water and I didn't think Costa could fail. Seriously, it sucks. I had four donuts for breakfast and two for lunch. It's all I've eaten today. I just added two sugars to my coffee and it tastes slightly better. I stole a ton of sugar packets as well, so I guess we're even.

Today I was going to go to the Guildhall Art Museum but it was closed for some reason. They had several entrances closed off around that whole area, and there were police or official people walking around. It's a bit chilly out and it feels fantastic. I also went to the university today and printed off my essay, which was so lame. I don't know if it was any good, but oh well.

Today was a solitary day and I'm very happy about it. I haven't written in a while. Oh, I also printed off pics of seahorses for my tat. Which I am for sure getting. I'm thinking I'll get it next month, because I'm fucking poor this month. I don't want to have any more things.

Travis likes me and I do not like him back. I started my period and it leaked a tiny bit on my sheets. I need to do laundry tomorrow.

Last night I ate a ton of shit and the whole day until like seven I had been trying to not overeat. I have to write a Film History essay and it's going to be so bad. It's due the Monday after next. Not excited.

I'm wearing my gray t-shirt dress and tall, black, wool socks. Everyone has been staring at my legs. Ha ha ha. Sawyer got a laptop for his birthday and I told him to get Skype so we can chat! Face to fuckin' face.

There's this deep sadness inside me that no male will ever explore. There's a crooked line of anxiety lodged in my heart and it will never be straightened out. Unless I cut to the core of it, unless I face it alone and vulnerable, which I cannot do. I need to do the things that I fear, I need to do what makes me anxious, I need to feel that anxiety fully.

I need to be hurt, I need someone to slap me in the face. I need a revolution. I need action when I'm incapable of moving, when I cannot decide my fate because worry cripples me. I need to be a part of something. I should count how many times I've said this. Inactivity = anxiety. Am I simply unwilling to participate??

Night slowly drips into the atmosphere, mixing with your exhaled smoke. You are a child and the wiser of the two. Another speaks of art and architecture. And Kurt Cobain's laughter, which is quite endearing. You only want to feel the texture of his voice when he's sick, or talk about people that aren't dead.

I don't want to go home I want this pencil to never stop sailing, smooth sailing failed poetry, neon vests and the wasted remains of everything we've seen, been, heard of, loved. Everything is gone or will be soon, the slice of flesh, the sting of silver sorrow, money, holidays, meaninglessness of titles, categories, descriptions, days, time, light, dark, noise, verbs, heat. It's all only brain waves struggling to keep moving, traveling, hoping to hold this energy inside, grasping when it fades,

choking on your breakfast, never hungry only desiring things that aren't meant to be, a sick confusion of right and wrong, the smell of literature, the only thing that's ever been right, if you decide right means good, but if you decide otherwise, what then? Does the world suddenly stop and spin the other way? Do we go hurtling through darkness until the moon is only a pinprick, until the sun disappears and we all die, shivering and lonely?

Yeah, we don't need any of this bullshit.

13 November 2011

Last night I dreamt that I met Harry McVeigh of White Lies in a bar. Like, I just saw him and went up to him and was like are you in the band White Lies? And he said yes, and the only thing I remember was that we were driving in a car listening to the radio and one of their songs came on and we were both like, "Oh my god!" And laughed. And then I slept in his bed but nothing happened, which I was glad of because I really wanted to get to know him, not just fuck him or something. And then I woke up and was really sad that it didn't happen. Because he is fucking sexy and I can't get over it.

Today I went to Liverpool Street station and tried to find this flower market and failed. So I went to a different market and then went to Foyle's, where I bought a book about existentialism for Sawyer for his birthday. I want to read it eventually. My lips are so chapped and chafed, and like crusty crust. Gross. I have been effectively procrastinating writing my essay. Fuck. Okay, well, I guess that is all.

15 November 2011

Ten minutes until Social Problems. Lame. Yesterday classes were alright. I worked out and tried to write my Film History essay but didn't get very far. I just can't concentrate when I try to write it and it's the worst thing ever. Boring as hell.

I started reading *Atlas Shrugged* by Ayn Rand and so far I like it. Descriptive, in-depth characterization, the works. I'm starting to part my hair in the middle and I'm growing out my bangs, and I actually like my hair, isn't that weird? I feel like I have nothing to say right now, just because I'm tired. My Econ teacher looks like Björk and I'm totally in love with her.

Undated

I'm always in the mood to eat and I don't want to be in that mood. I hate food, it's just another trap the world has set for my weakling mind and I always succumb.

You repulse me I am repulsed by anyone who's interested I'm suspicious of your ulterior motives everyone has these motives they're going to hurt me they're going to take advantage they're going to take my love unwillingly I'll never give it up I'll never trust I'll never trust or give or love

I don't want you I don't want to sleep I don't want to commit to anything I can't get out of, eye contact is too much it's too intimate a connection I can hear everything you're thinking in your eyes

£ £ £uck

17 November 2011

Yesterday Sakura and I went to this Christmas market thing on Marylebone Street and it was soooo cool! We got a ton of free samples, it was basically my lunch/dinner. Sweet. Then I wrote the shit out of my Film History essay, it's basically done. I don't know if it is good though, probably not.

My nails are getting longer because I painted the tips black and I don't bite them in order to preserve the polish. They look fucking cool in my opinion.

I think today I am going to go look at the Tower of London, but not go inside because you have to pay. Because I don't have to do anything today, wooo. I don't know what else, I feel weird and can't concentrate.

Not cool: computer on the fritz, running out of fake sugar, cigarettes, money, patience, not getting Mom's package, feeling bloated, darkness before five p.m., running out of glue, not having tape, not being attracted to anyone, trying and failing to top up my motherfucking phone, not having service and not knowing why, having to call those people back, having to figure out logistics for EVERYTHING, running out of batteries, bananas, food in general, not having money for alcohol, waking up late and wasting the daylight, being tired all the time, not knowing what I want

MY FUCKING ASSHOLE COMPUTER I'M GOING TO KILL EVERYONE!

18 November 2011

I am so motherfucking anxious right now. I feel hopeless and like nothing I want will ever work out because I'm too afraid to talk to people.

I need someone impulsive and reckless and unconventional and obsessed with death and artistic and skinny and contradictory and self-destructive. I need to feel something. I want someone angry and scared.*

I'm scared to call those people about working at the Summer Olympics, which I realized I don't think I mentioned before. I might work them because they are in London next year and they are going to need a ton of people so I could totally do it! But my anxiety about phones is prohibiting me from pursuing this. Fuck my life.

[*Ana: You don't actually want this unless it is functioning productively and doesn't manifest negatively towards you. You already have Saturn, what more could you want? You want a mirror, you want someone to understand. You don't want someone that needs fixing. –J.]

20 November 2011

Today is Sawyer's birthday. Today Sakura and I went to this art market by Hyde Park and it was neat. I wrote to Grandma and worked out. I feel okay, I think. I Skyped Jenna and my parents for a little bit. I painted my toenails black. I'm in the lounge now. I was looking at my hearts on weheartit.com and finding inspiration.

Yesterday and the day before I didn't feel very good. Just super anxious and unreal and unsafe, in danger. It felt bad. But we went to the Tate Modern and it was pretty sweet. We also went to one of Sakura's friend's, like, dance/music performance, and it was basically all black people. The performance was so bad, like even the sound was all crackly and stuff. And I felt gross and fat (not because of the performance or the people) so I left early and got groceries.

I have been eating everyone's food from the kitchen because everyone is gone to Wales and Amsterdam. Ha. I think I'm just going to do that on a regular basis because I hate them all. It's their own fault because they don't lock their motherfucking cupboards and shit (they have locks, which is nice).

I haven't felt like a real person for the last couple of days, and it's because I feel like I need to get a job and support myself. It's just this weird irrational thought that's been pervading my mind. But I decided that I want to be a waitress.* I don't know why but I feel like that would be cool. I just get good vibes from that idea. I dunno.

[*Ana: You do NOT want to be a waitress. Holy shit. That would be the worst job in the entire world for you. –J.]

Tomorrow I have classes and it's going to be lame. I don't really like my classes. They are okay but I don't give a shit about them. Whatever.

Last night Sakura and I went to Brick Lane because we had never been there at night. We went to the Big Chill Bar and there were a ton of creative people. There was a girl from southern England who didn't wear a shirt and had long dreads and a half shaved head, and I was so jealous of her life. She said she'd grown up on farms and she loved it, and I was so jealous. I feel like there are so many interesting people, and how will I meet them? Because you can't seriously meet someone at a bar, you know? The people in my classes aren't cool. There's no one I want to know everything about, or that looks super eclectic and revolutionary.* Ugh.

[*Ana: You can't determine if someone is eclectic/revolutionary just by how they look or dress. Often the people that look the most interesting are actually the most stupid and boring and judgmental and ignorant. It's weird how that works but it's true. Just to make things even more difficult for you, the cool people are often incognito. –J.]

Things to be excited about: growing out my nails, reading *Atlas Shrugged*, hair longer and parted in the middle, a package from home coming soon, wearing the clothes that I own, loving all the things I have and not needing anything else, not being a virgin, theft, using things up and throwing them away, not having homework for a while, coffee, dying my hair soon, this notebook, my graph paper notebooks, poetry, my watch, guys thinking I'm attractive even though I'm actually super ugly in real life.

21 November 2011

Last night while lying in bed I was thinking about my anxiety, and I was realizing that there SERIOUSLY is no reason to be anxious. Like, I'm not in danger. No one is going to hurt me. And so what if I'm spending my parents' money? So what if I have to rely on them still? They are my parents, they brought me into this world, they *should* be taking care of me, so I don't have to feel guilty or worry about it.

Also, young people in Britain rely on their parents for much longer than people in America, so it's not like I'm abnormal or something. I think guilt might be the source of my anxiety.* I feel like I should be doing all these things or else I'm a bad person. It's just completely unnecessary. And fucked.

[*Ana: Bro, that's the Saturn shit. –J.]

Delicious things: jam filled donuts, flaky pastries, ice cream from McDonald's, Costa motherfucking coffee, blood, urine, shit, especially when all mixed together, vomit, too.

The other day Sakura and I were walking to our tube station in the underground and we saw this girl lying on the ground in her own vomit. She was so drunk and her friend was trying to help her, and a security woman was calling for someone to clean it up. And I couldn't get the picture out of my head.

23 November 2011

I'm acquiring a cough. Not good. A lot of people are sick though, so it's alright. Last night I dreamt that Sakura, who was at the same time Kan, died, and it was HORRIBLE. I cried like the whole time in my dream. I don't know what else.

Classes were long and horrible but I made it through. Kan typed a long-ass entry on our Kana blog and it was the best part of my day yesterday. I also Skyped her and Sawyer/Lacy yesterday, which was nice. I feel like I'm online way too much and it makes my brain hurt. Bleh.

Right now I'm drinking coffee and eating a banana with peanut butter. I already had a donut. This is breakfast. I need some good vibes. Right now I don't think I feel anything. Hmm. Today is slightly overcast, but it's just a super thin layer of cloud over the sky and you can still see blue. Yesterday was extremely overcast and I loved it.

I think I want to (need to?) have an alone day where I go to a coffee shop and study or read *Atlas Shrugged*. Today Sakura and I are going to Portobello Road to see if there is an antiques market or something. I am going to get ready now, I guess.

Alright. Portobello Road/Notting Hill was pretty sweet. We went to an antiques market, didn't buy anything. I also worked out. I think Sakura has class tomorrow so I am going to go wander around the Barbican because I have no idea what that even is, haha.

I am irritated with Travis. I was Facebook chatting him and he asked me if I told anyone that we fucked (OMG DID I TELL YOU?), and I was like, "Kan." And he told all the guys on our floor when they were in Amsterdam. Which is fine, I don't care if people know, it just makes me feel like they all think Travis and I have this thing, which we don't. Or that we like each other a lot and are like a unit, like Lauren and Ben or Chris and Carla or Hannah and JR. And we're not, and I don't want to be. So that's just annoying.

And I was like, "It's okay, I don't care." And he was like, "No, I know you care, you're self-conscious." And I was like, "No, I really don't care." And he was like, "It's okay, I know you're insecure." And that made me so angry. First of all because he acts like he knows me. Like, really knows me, like to the extent that Kan knows me. And he absolutely does not. He may know particular things that I've told him (while drunk) but he does not know by experience.

And to call someone insecure (even if they are) is RUDE. AND, I am not ALWAYS insecure. That is a small aspect of my personality partly because I'm hyper self-critical.* But I'm only insecure around some people, in particular situations. I *never* feel or have felt insecure around Travis. Because I know that I'm cooler, more interesting, more intelligent, and less awkward than him. So for him to say that is just dumb. Especially when he has not seen it or experienced it himself.

[*Ana: Yes, hyper self-critical and intensely self-aware, as well as extraordinarily introverted. Introverted to the point where talking quickly becomes physically draining, almost exhausting, especially when it is about superficial bullshit that isn't intellectual. –J.]

So basically I am not attracted to him at all anymore. I was actually only attracted to him when I was drunk, so that's not even saying much. I hate people that tell everyone about their sexual lives! That's so annoying. It just bugs the shit out of me because it's like drama or high school or immaturity. It's like making sex this crazy experience when it's just whatever. It's not a big deal so why tell everybody? I don't know.

I just feel like they all have this image of Travis and I fucking in their heads and that makes me feel so gross and uncomfortable. God, whatever, this is so lame. I don't know why I am ranting about this because it doesn't even matter and I don't care about what Travis thinks of me, because whatever it is, it's wrong. Plus, I can't take him seriously ever because he's too sarcastic. And not sensitive and not even my type! Haha wtf goodnight.

24 November 2011

Barbican Centre. Costa hot chocolate. Fountains. Green, dark water amidst an explosion of buildings. City of London School for Girls, plants hanging from the balconies of apartments, things I shouldn't buy, things I promise myself I won't buy, being coldish but it feels so GOOD, the wind as slightly irritating but endured.

IT'S OKAY. WHATEVER HAPPENS, IT'S OKAY.

Maybe my anxiety is caused by the system, by society, capitalism, the government, the masses, the majority, the rules, the man.

The ephemeral quality of all things in this life. That is what I fear.

This is peaceful, this is wonderful, this is calm. The slapping sounds of white water, curtained windows, potted plants, people on the other side of transparent glass, silent, watchful, gazing. I'm free here, I'm safe, I'm not trapped in the boxes I create in my mind.

I want immortality, perfection, permanence, security, the constant stability of sanity, to keep everything remembered forever, never forgotten…but truly I don't want any of these things. I'll get bored and feel trapped, I'm contradicting myself, fucking up the harmony or unity I might have had in another life, why do my cigarettes always burn out in the end, withering into ashes, reflecting my disarray, my ineptitude at making things last, at enjoying what I wanted and received, at loving everything about my existence in any given moment.

To be in love with one's existence, how can it be? How do you get to that point? I want to use things up and discard them, but I can't let them go, I need to save them I need to feel them I need to be them.

I don't want anything unless it's perfect, I can't stand it when it's less than my ideal, it has to be art, it has to be the unity of two minds, the corpus callosum feeding me and my other half, holding us together I don't want short hair and black pea coats and business shoes. I want violence and lust and abstractions and fibers of insane brilliance and fucking despair.

I want odd jobs and temp jobs and photographs and Splenda. I want to throw out my clothes, the colours of fall, the lights reflecting in your eyes and in the windows of the skyscrapers. I need your fingernails to be dirty, I need you to be skinny and not tall. I need your clothes to be ripped I need you to have cuts on your arms and tattoos I need you to look like me, I'm narcissistic as fuck I can only love myself and the texture of acrylics. And pigeons that limp, and the sooty dustiness of dusk, layers of clouds, fabric old and worn, the fabrics of a historical beauty, a vintage desire, a reputation of fashion,

a wasted youth, wasted time, wasted movement, meaningless gestures, schizophrenic desires, pain colored in the pages of a magazine, in the margins of a book, hidden in the strands of your hair, under your lipstick, stained into the porcelain of your teacups, melted into your bleeding heart, stapled into the wooden walls of your picturesque frame, the boards of your safe house, the cans of your spaghetti, the meat on your bones, licking the strips of your tendons with white hot flame, burning into a spent soul,

tired of living and waiting for nothing, trying uselessly to find meaning in a chaotic, hostile world, an empty world of hopelessness, of terrible beauty, of exhaustion.

I want to do something I've never done before, I want to wear something I've never worn before, I want to style my hair a new way.

Back at the dorms. I think one of my favorite pastimes would have to be stealing other people's food from the kitchen. Seriously, most fun thing ever. Because they totally deserve it for not locking their cupboards and for being lame Americans. Anyway, I just get a rush from doing it and it makes me feel like James Bond.

I need to go to sleep even if I am not that tired because I'm getting up at seven so I can go do that Olympics screening thing, to see if I can work during the summer.

Oh wait, I forgot to say that Sakura and I went to the Wellcome Collection, a free art museum thing, and it was soooo fucking cool. Upstairs is all about medicine and anatomy and stuff, and I was reading this graphic novel about mental disorders, and it was super interesting and made me feel like things would be okay. Because I know other people feel the same. And tons of people are worse off than me! Like, they have more anxiety than me, even if they are better off than me or the same as me.

I think today was really good. I got to be alone and find some calm, and I wrote a ton and that was cathartic, and I saw a lot of creative things. I felt like I was creative as well, so that was wonderful. I just felt okay. I guess that's all that matters. I dunno.

I just finished Skyping my fam, plus my aunt and uncle, Grandma, and Lacy. It's midnight here and like four p.m. there. They are drinking beer before eating Thanksgiving dinner. I loved seeing and talking with them. Anyway, I think now I will finally go to bed.

25 November 2011

The flickering yellow light in a red telephone booth

The piercing stares of lost souls, searching and curious

Crackling dried up leaves, scuttling across the ground

Little fountains in Russell Square

Everything is still green and beautiful, unlike Boise in the fall

The pointed spires of a lost generation

Your days are numbered

THINGS I FEAR I'LL NEVER DO:

My twisted fucker love, I'm worried I'm getting dumber, I'm worried I'm not learning anything, I'll always find something to worry about, I'm worried I'll never get a job, I'll never be able to support myself, I'll never find love because there will always be someone better than the person I'm with, I'll never publish a book because I don't know how to start, I'll never feel safe, ever.

Because there's always that fucking silky black anxiety hovering over me. Sometimes it drifts off for a while, sometimes it chokes me, almost suffocating, leaving me immobile and nervous and alone, and knowing I'm not real, knowing I'm meaningless and not actually there.

I can't remember the things that have happened to me, I can't figure out if what I create is good quality. I can't figure out if my friends are right for me, if they are the people I'm supposed to have met, I can't concentrate anymore, I can only procrastinate, I can't grasp the power of money, I feel like I'm the only person that worries about this shit but I know I'm not.

I'll never feel like life is worth living, for more than a day or two. I'll never do things fully, completely, only half-assed and bullshitted. I can't even cut myself with any passion. I only do it a little bit, I can't let the blood really flow, am I scared of pain? I'll never know.

What I want: Costa and *Atlas Shrugged* and a lot of free time, a library to check out books, infinite fake sugar, someone to exploit but in a good way, to smoke a lot of cigarettes inside a house/apartment.

Accepting the ephemeral quality of life, rather than fearing it. Adoring it rather than feeling anxious. Alone? Is today an "alone and happy about it" day?

Just to let you know, cutting releases tension.

Today was basically the best day ever. The universe was actually NOT an asshole to me! I had that thing with the summer Olympic people, and it was totally fine, and I'm pretty sure I got the job. I feel like everyone did if they didn't prove to be an idiot. There's a possibility that I could work like all summer. And they're paying around eight pounds an hour. That's so much! At least when you convert it to dollars…

Anyway, I'm just really excited and I hope it works and that I actually do get the job. Also, I got there way early because I wanted to make sure I found the place on time, and it actually started 30 minutes before I thought I had to be there, but I was still a bit early. So that was lucky!

I didn't spend any money today, and I visited a Gandhi memorial in this park by Eustan Station, and these BBC people interviewed me about trees, haha. So maybe I will be on TV somewhere. All day I didn't feel anxious, and I felt fine talking to people. AND I had to call this place to get a National Identity number so I can work here, and I got it without any problems, which is insane because there are always problems for me! Especially with phones and calling people. And it was totally fine.

At nine tonight I am going to go to a bar and meet this Tyrone guy that started talking to me on the street the other day. Did I mention him? I don't think I did. He is from South Africa, but is white. I don't know what will happen but I hope it goes well, because today was a good day and I want it to be wholly good, not shitty at the end. I feel like he just wants to fuck me, hmm. Probably, he's a man. I don't know if I want to fuck him or not. Whatever. Okay, that is all.

26 November 2011

Soul, feathers, interest, shells, soap, strokes, texture, bubbles, fur, disease, music, time, unhappiness, pastries, sex, lines, videos, practice, inhale, mist, beaches, loneliness, vertigo, places. Something's missing.

Undated

Notes: every man thinks I'm special, that I am the one, that somehow I'm different than all the others. And I reject them, I always reject them and throw them away because they are never the right one for me, and I know I'm not the one for them.

Questions to ask people: Do you know what your life is for? Are you happy, content? Where do you want to live when you're older? Where are the places you've been? Favorite?

Oh, this infinite space.

The ink smooth and thick and luscious, falling out of my pen, sliding all over the lines, creeping and winking and licking and working. Reading my mind, my thoughts, my lusts, my quirks and hates and fucks.

Doing what nobody expects, rejecting society, changing your opinions and preferences but not on purpose, it just sneaks up on you, insidiously. Throwing things away, recycling this action, this memory, this regret, this reluctance, this humiliation: all of it thrown into oblivion, ending up as dust and dirt, related to a gravestone, forgotten, stupid, inane, unlovable

wretched, horrid, faulty, broken, lost in space and time

Sexual: eyebrow rings, quiet/thoughtful, writes, makes things, destructive, has good grammar, likes to read and drink coffee, piercings and tattoos – I love that shit – draws me.

27 November 2011

Okay, so…I fucked Tyrone. A lot. And in the morning he came on my back. HAHA what the fuck? I dunno. He cleaned it off though, so it was okay. And he bought me breakfast, so that was cool. We went bar hopping and it was actually really fun! He is funny, like he kind of reminds me of a more mature Calvin, except that he listens to what you say and looks kind of like he should be on *Jersey Shore*, haha.

I left my phone at his place on accident so I will see him again in order to get it back, but I dunno if I'll see him again after that. Because I think he's kind of a player, which is fine with me because I'm a player as well. I just didn't find him particularly intriguing or intellectual and the sex was boring. I mean, he had a great time, but I didn't come or even find it that pleasurable. It's kind of like someone is just continually shoving/pushing you and it gets really boring and tiring after a while.

Today I went to Spitalfields Market, Brick Lane, and the Sunday Upmarket in Brick Lane, all in search of that Kurt Cobain shirt I want, but I had no luck. I think I'm going to look for it in Camden. I dunno. My jaws are tired from chewing gum all day.

The monster within only comes out at night.

Undated but possibly
27 November 2011

not having a phone, pencil sharpeners, technological difficulties, sitting in the shower, flavored coffee creamer, PMS, Carmex, packages from home, creative websites, my brain's imminent implosion, fully charged batteries, stores, paper as a vessel for catharsis, ringing ears, texture of paint, car keys, pastries, drawings of people I know, the smooth blackness of this Sharpie as comparable to my soul and the tips of my nails and the color of my iPod, maps, collections, vibes, choosing what to wear, looking for inspiration, spying on people,

seeing guys check out my legs, plum-stained lips, plans, morning messiness, the sleep in your eyes and hair, the overcast skies reflected in your mug, rubber bands, school supplies and stationery stores, not having a purpose, bracelets, rings, not doing homework, chocolate, engravings in wood or cement, stray hairs, down coats, cobblestone roads and how right that is, how good that is, how the eccentricity of Europe is embraced, how it's NORMAL, the feeling of anticipation while getting film developed, taking naps and not being able to sleep at night,

watching movies you've already seen, certain people's handwriting as elegant and beautiful, museums when it's raining, not wearing a bra, loops and curves, staying up late, maturing, growing older, changing your mind, feeling that it's okay to make mistakes, headaches, dehydration, being sexually active, body mist, video games, moccasins, drugs, wanting to do more drugs, looking rich but not being rich at all, looking homeless but not being homeless, puppies, dogs, clear tape, collages, coffee shops, Christmas drinks at coffee shops,

not feeling like it's Christmastime, being irritable, not knowing what to say, knowing someone thinks you're attractive, being in love with a person because of his *mind*, because of what he says, because of what he believes, socks, rooms, cleaning your piercings, having piercings, pills, tampons, boredom, wandering, money, temporary jobs, odd jobs, walking up the stairs, walking down the stairs, the smell of hairspray, the smell of memories, cheap food, flyers, oily skin, nothing to say, repeating myself,

HONEY CHEESE BUTTER BREAD I AM KINDA OVERFED

Don't eat when you're not hungry! FUCKIN' HELL

28 November 2011

Today I got my phone back from Tyrone and we went to Greg's (the same place as the place we got pastries at on Saturday morning) and he bought me a pizza thing because he's obsessed with them. I thought he was just going to give me my phone and then peace out, so it was cool that we hung out. I can't figure out his intentions, because I don't understand how someone like him would like someone like me. We just don't seem compatible in my mind.

I left Film History today super early and came home and took a nap. Then I worked out and hung out with Sakura in the lounge. Now I'm about to eat pasta. So that was my day. Pretty lame, I suppose. Okay, that's all.

29 November 2011

Annoying things: not getting Mom's package, not having tape or glue, doing the same shit every day, staring at the computer screen for hours, not having any inspiration, not having as many options as America, not wanting to go back to Idaho but wanting to go back to America.

I'm just extremely stressed out by the lack of interesting people around me. And by wanting to eat everything I see. And by the idea that getting pregnant is actually a possibility in the un-virgin girl's life. And by hating my classes, and by not having a job, and by having a job, and by being human, being alive, enduring this worthless, meaningless shit called "existence."

Things that make me like the people in the books and movies: riding the tube always and getting occasional headaches from it, fucking a person I met on the street, working a temp job at the university, most likely working at the Summer Olympics, stealing people's food from the kitchen, living in London, going places alone, being obsessed with coffee, writing this list under the lamp light while drinking a cup of tea, being irritable and wanting to escape everyone, skipping class.

30 November 2011

It's 9:45 a.m. and I'm doing this room auditor job thing I got through the university. It's the best job ever. All I do is count people in classrooms (and today there is no one because of a strike or something) and then hang out until the next hour to do it again. It only takes like 20 minutes.

So right now I'm in the café downstairs, which I didn't know existed before today, and I have about 25 minutes to waste until I have to count people again. And they'll probs be all zeros again.

It's quite peaceful here, I love it. The lights are dim and the furniture is all pastel colored. I'm totally getting paid to sit around. Haha fucking legit. This is what life is supposed to be like.

The guy that gave me the room audit sheets was so cute! He had a British accent and pierced ears and was wearing a flannel and was so nice, and looked genuine. Totally my type. Which is weird because he is legit the first person I've seen that has been my type, or the closest to a type that I could call mine.

I'm thinking about taking a nap after my second shift. I have my phone to set an alarm. That would make the time go by faster. Okay, well, I guess that's all for now…

It's 12:05 p.m. now. I took a nap and did my third audit and I'm in the café again. I made a list of things I want to do eventually and I feel like my life is a bit more organized. In a couple minutes I'm going to do my last audit, and then wait around until one p.m. so I get paid for the whole time.

This pen, the light falling across my hand, the silkiness of my hair, not writing thoughts solely in one particular journal, the half ponytail bun thing that European girls do to their hair, realizing that people over here are not necessarily better than the people in America, realizing how much of a privilege living in America actually is, watching movies while working out, HAVING HEADPHONES FINALLY, reading past thoughts and feeling the same way still, having the same desires, having hair that I actually like for once in my life, sleeping during my three-day temp job HAHA, long nails, long nails, naps with the lights on, not feeling like I want to eat everything, cheap pastries,

01 December 2011

Last night Sakura and I went to Brick Lane to see this art supply store she found, it was pretty sweet. I found this green journal thing that I want to use for my next journal, when I run out of things to write on. We also went to this vintage department store called Blitz and it was sooo cool, and they had cheap books for sale that I wanted to buy. I wanted to buy everything. But I didn't, so that's good.

I also worked out last night while watching a movie, because I finally got headphones in the mail. Glorious. They are really nice, too. Now I can go on runs outside because my headphones won't fall out of my ears like the earbuds do.

I'm in the café waiting to do my last audit. It's almost four p.m. I'm done in an hour. I think it feels safe in here because it's dark. I don't want to go back to the dorms. I just realized that right now. I'm getting so annoyed with it, especially with the people on my floor. Bleh. It's all just bleh bleh bleh.

Things: flat hair, writing in pencil, safety under dim lights, to-do lists, slight anxiety with no cause, thinking you have no life because there's no point to life, shouldn't your job be your life? Because you're going to be involved with that for most of your life, in order to pay your motherfucking bills. Fuck society, fuck everyone.

I think I'm fat and ugly.

02 December 2011

Last day of "work." Today has been really good, I like myself. I got up at nine and had coffee and got ready, then mailed Sawyer's package and went to the university to see if they had any London Eye tickets left. Which they didn't, but that's okay because Kan is coming to visit me and gets here that day and I'll get to do it in the spring anyway.

Then I had a ton of time before work so I walked around in the sunny, crisp, brisk, autumn air, and it was so lovely and beautiful. The cold made me feel fresh and alive. I discovered many parks and gardens and interesting places, and I sat in Finsbury Park for a while and watched these goofy guys play tennis. They sucked and it was awesome. Haha.

I'm at work now and it's gone by so quickly. I brought my computer and have been sorting out emails and to-dos and such things. Also, the guy that works at the café became my friend and he paid for my mocha when I ordered it. So kind! He is from Sierra Leone and his name is Philip.

Safety is a state of mind.

Lately I have just been feeling so much more socially competent, and better at life shit. Like getting jobs and figuring out stuff, like getting a national insurance number. I like it a lot because it makes me feel like a real person and in turn I like myself more. It's strange.

Today I was thinking about how I live in London, and how it's the biggest city in motherfucking EUROPE. And how I have it all figured out, like how it all works. Not *all*, but a lot. It's just so crazy to me, because I always thought my life was so fucking boring and stupid, because I lived in Idaho, but now I have a fresh perspective and experience and I like being from America. I just feel like I know how the world works now, to a greater depth than before, at least. Obviously I don't know everything.

Today I have vibes of well-being, and I know it won't last forever but it's nice that I have it now. The total pay of these three days of work is £99.60. YES. That's $156.56. I feel so accomplished. Okay, I'm leaving because I have to pee like a motherfucker.

04 December 2011

Today I want to go to the Museum of London. I am supposed to start my period soon and I am paranoid as fuck that I'm pregnant. Last night I ate so much shit, and I watched *The Bourne Identity*, and I'm still waiting for that to happen to me – you know, hot guy takes loner girl on an insane adventure.

I don't know what else to say. Kan comes in less than two weeks. Crazy. Mom's package FINALLY got here, yippee.

I want to be behind the scenes of something important, meaningful.

05 December 2011

I'm supposed to be in Film History right now but I woke up too late to make it on time so I decided to skip. Also, it's pointless anyway because all I have to do for the class is write an essay, and I'm going to write it on something we've already learned. So it's just dumb.

I just saw my Film History assistant teacher. I am not making eye contact. He is in the café and I am also in the café…

Okay, he is gone now. I dunno if he saw me. Haha fuck. I think I'm gonna go to the Southbank Centre and hang out and do homework, like research essay shit. Okay, yeah, I'm totes going to do that! Woo.

I am on my period and I am feeling irritable, tired, bored, indecisive, and hungry. But I don't want to go back to the dorms because I hate it. I drank too much water so I have to pee like every five seconds. Bleh. I feel so BLEH. Ugh, I hate it. Oh, I also feel bloated as well, and farty and fat. Oh my gross.

Hopeless, despair, futility of life.

THINGS THAT EXIST:

tar, tired, holes in socks, cough drops, trying to avoid the computer, headaches and coffee as a solution to them, reading at a desk – how are you supposed to sit when reading?

going to class as a futile effort when I already know what homework I have to do, and it concerns material we've already learned,

snacking, craving,

too many people, too much noise, too much stimuli, smoke, movements, smells, lights, silence as exotic, as a heavy luster coating particular rooms, my room, the way your tongue feels when you eat too much candy, how it doesn't go away because you don't stop eating candy, essays, needing intellectual endeavors to feel purposeful, how it's satisfying to complete homework in a quiet, dim coffee shop, the blinking lights of planes, the lights of buildings highlighted against a night sky, how I'm a part of that light while writing this, how others have probably thought of that before

06 December 2011

12 minutes until Social Problems. I'm drinking a hot chocolate I got from Philip. He is busy so I didn't really get to talk to him. Last night I went to bed at 9:56, and I feel well rested. I think. Class is going to be dreadful, only because it's pointless. I think I should work out tonight. *Atlas Shrugged* is a wonderful book. Whoa, everything I say is random as shit.

07 December 2011

This is the perfect time in my life to do whatever I want and not be held down. No boyfriend, job, or other ties to limit the possibilities. I'm in Europe, I yearn to explore, to discover other ways of living, to realize and reevaluate my priorities and values and desires, to figure out exactly what I want to do, and where, if I ever desire, to settle down and have a job.

Tattoos as works of art, the sound of pencil on paper as music, simple joys as complex and meaningful pleasures, PERSPECTIVES, walking instead of driving, public transportation.

What I want: To work odd jobs, to never stay in one place for longer than a couple years, to have a tiny cheap-ass home with only the essentials, to not own very many things (clothes, jewelry, etc.), to have adventures, to work out, to not eat a shit-ton, to drink coffee out of a chipped old mug, to have multiple opportunities for artistic outlets, to share experiences, to have an understanding, a connection, with another, to not be tied down, to not be faithful or loyal to only one, but to have respect for all associates, to use the materials directly at hand, to have a project, to be part of a project that is important that I can invest my time in and that does not seem pointless to me, to VALUE something as worthwhile, to read when bored.

08 December 2011

I am alone in my room, it's 12:45 p.m. I'm drinking coffee. It's gray outside and windy. I'm going to go to Camden today and buy Christmas presents for my family. I watched *Boondock Saints* while working out yesterday and the day before, and I cannot get over how sexy they are, it's unbelievable. Especially Norman Reedus. His voice is the BEST.

Oh, we went to Ministry of Sound Tuesday night, it was cool. I made out with this random guy on the dance floor in front of everyone from my floor and it was awesome. Travis saw too, and then at like four in the morning him and I fucked in the stairwell at the dorms. Haha it was fucking awesome. I am still on my period and was at the time that we fucked, but it was the very beginning so nothing was happening. Like, it had already started but at that time there was no blood. Haha what the fuck I am gross. He wore a condom and we left it in the stairwell, it's probs still there. Um, gross.

We have fruit flies in our room because Moe is deranged. She keeps her rotting bananas in here, and throws her peels out in here rather than in the kitchen. Dumb.

Kan comes next week! So excite. Nothing else to say. Why can I never remember what I want to express when I get the opportunity to express it?

09 December 2011

I accomplished a lot today! I went to the British Library and took a few notes on *The Blue Angel* for Film History, and then went to Sainsbury's for a couple groceries. Then I went to Kensington Gardens/Palace/Park and to the Serpentine Gallery in Hyde Park, which was kind of lame except for this one installation that was in a dark room. There were a ton of wires or strings at angles going up to the ceiling. They were under this golden warm light, and it was really pretty. Angular, crisscrossing, geometric. I dunno how they put it together because the strings were all perfectly straight but were intertwined kind of. I dunno, hard to explain.

Anyway, now I am in Café Nero and I got a dark chocolate mocha, which was okay but not my favorite. It was one of the holiday special things. Today is Friday and the people on my floor are going to Koko. I am not going because it costs like seven pounds. So I want to go somewhere else tonight, like just walk around a really populated area, like Piccadilly Circus or something. Or maybe I'll go to Primark because I haven't been yet. I don't really want to buy anything though…hmm.

Moe and I are going to go to this chocolate festival thing tomorrow morning. I think it's this huge event. Hopefully we will get free samples.

I'm leaving because this guy decided to sit right next to me and he is invading my space. And he is loud and gross.

10 December 2011

So last night I ended up just hanging out in my room. I started watching this movie called *We Need to Talk about Kevin* online and it made me feel uncomfortable. I haven't finished it yet.

Today we went to the chocolate festival, which was super crowded and pretty small, but we got a few samples so it was cool. Then Moe and I parted ways and I walked past the London Eye and across the bridge and to the Houses of Parliament, to the park by Parliament, and by Westminster Abbey, all the way to Victoria Station. I bought some donuts at Sainsbury's for 69 pence. I bought Dad a mug and socks for

Christmas. I think I am done with Xmas shopping. Then I worked out and now I am in the lounge with Sakura, as per usual.

Undated

shifting secret movements, "bad places" in your mind and how scary that is, all the things I don't remember, expectation, anticipation, the meaning held by particular sounds, tones, how something can mean the world to one person and nothing to another, how that seems terribly tragic,

12 December 2011

class, excitement/anticipation, carefree feelings concerning hunger and places to sleep, not hungry at all, the end of something, goodbyes as welcome and good because I don't care about the people I'm saying goodbye to, doors opening, new beginnings, new people, new things to do, new explorations and adventures and conversations, not feeling anxious about people, maybe just frustrated because people don't get it and that makes them annoying and stupid, not me,

14 December 2011

Kan is finally here! Yesterday she got here around 2:45 p.m., but my phone had no service so she waited in the dorm lobby for an hour until I went down at 3:45 to pick her up at King's Cross, because that's when I thought her train got here.

Yesterday we went to the study abroad dinner thing to celebrate the end of the semester, but we didn't go to the London Eye. We sat with Taiki and Victoria and it was funny. I also got a paper plate award from these two guys from my floor that were giving everyone awards, for being the "Travis Tamer." Hahaha fucking dumb.

We walked across Westminster Bridge to Houses of Parliament, took the tube back to the dorms, and then went to Piccadilly Circus and Trafalgar

Square in the dark and took a ton of pictures. And climbed up to where the lions are.

This morning I woke at 8:30, Kan woke earlier, and we ate breakfast and went to St. James' Park and Buckingham Palace. Now we are chilling at Eat. It's so crazy that she is actually here. Like, my worlds are colliding, I love when that shit happens. I think we might get tats in Brick Lane today, I hope it works out. It's so wonderful that Kan is here. London is our playground. Our motherfucking playground.

15 December 2011

Things: a slow uneasiness, insidious, thinking I'm fat and ugly, red face, comparing myself. I hate when I do that…

We are hanging out in Costa right now. I am drinking a mint hot chocolate which is to die for, and Kan is drinking a caramel mocha. We are attempting to use the free wifi but it's super slow. She needs to upload pics and I am going to read *Atlas Shrugged.*

This morning we went on a run to Regent's Park and it was the first time I've gone on a run in forever. I was so tired. I want to start running more often.

Last night we went to the 24-hour Beigel Bake at Brick Lane, and went into Rough Trade and The Big Chill bar, so cool. We didn't get tats, but I found a place in the West End online that I want to go to, so I think we'll go there today and make an appointment or something. I really want some seahorses! I'm dying to get them. Well, I dunno what else.

17 December 2011

Alright, so many things have happened! I got my seahorse tats!! At this place by the intersection of Charing Cross and Shaftesbury Avenue. So tight. It cost £100, bleh. And it hurt like a motherfucker. But I love them!

Then we went to Club 333 with the people on my floor, but actually we didn't hang out with them at all. Kan and I got super wasted and made out with a ton of guys. I made out with at least four different guys. And Kan and I also made out with each other hahaha. We took a cab home that some random guy paid for. Kan went home with him and came back to the dorms at like eight in the morning. We also had one shot of 80% alcohol at the bar and we got sooo wasted. It was seriously the best thing ever, one of the best nights out I've had in London.

Yesterday we went to Chapel Market and the cool paper store in Angel, and then to Cool Britannia by Piccadilly Circus. I got a British flag and a small towel to bring traveling. It has the Brit flag on it and a side view of the Queen in black. Tite.

Besides that we didn't really do anything. We started packing…I check out tomorrow at 10 a.m. for winter break. We are going to travel a bit! We will use the dorm's storage, and since we don't leave till Tuesday we are going to be Sakura's guests and sleep in her roommate's bed because she is already gone. So everything will work out!

Oh, also, yesterday I took some clothes from the clothes recycling point at the dorm, and I got this awesome green jacket. I think I'm going to wear it on our travels. So excited.

OH, WHITE LIES IS TONIGHT! I can't wait, I am so in love with them. We might drink before we go; I stole a shit-ton of alcohol from the kitchen because everyone left their shit. So, yeah. We've stocked up on food…now we are at Café Nero. I had a delicious hot chocolate. And that is all.

19 December 2011

White Lies was fucking sublime. I loved it, they are so good live. At the end there was confetti and we were jumping to catch it, and I have a couple pieces I saved. We drank and it was weird because I didn't feel that drunk so I kept taking shots in the bathroom, and then the next morning was so shitty.

I had to get up at like 8:30 and pack the rest of my shit and get out of my room and move shit to storage, and move shit to Sakura's room because we are staying here until our flight on Tuesday (tomorrow). I was hungover and felt like shit and stressed because my card to get into the building was going to stop working at 10. And you can only have one overnight guest so we had to find a random person that would let me use their pass. It's just been kind of a hassle and has tired me out. So yesterday I just slept all day after we figured out our shit, and it felt amazing.

Today I woke at 12:30 and we went to Spitalfields Market. I took a nap when we got back because I felt shitty. Like, mentally. I dunno. I just feel weird because I don't have my own room anymore and I feel homeless. And I feel like the Kana connection isn't as strong anymore, and I have no idea. I just feel like Kan is kind of mean, almost. Like, she has a snappy reply to what I say all the time, and is super easily irritated and quick to argue or bicker with me. I don't get it. It's making me sad and uncomfortable and weird.

Because Kan should make me feel safe; she's my best friend. But lately I just don't want to tell her how I feel about anything because she'll act like I shouldn't feel that way or act like it's dumb or that there's no reason to feel that way. It's just so strange and it sucks, and today I just wanted to not exist, so I took a nap for a few hours. I was going to work out, but that never happened. Kan was going to work out as well but that didn't happen either.

She is actually sleeping right now. She started taking a nap while I was asleep. Now it's 11:30 p.m. and she'll probs wake up at like six again, but that's good because we have to figure out how to get to the airport before 10 a.m. And put the rest of our shit in storage.

I need to go to Sainsbury's, or Boots. I just realized I could go to Boots in the morning because there's one in King's Cross. Perf. I need travel bottle/container things for face wash and toothpaste.

I feel like Kan and I aren't on the same page and it makes me feel so uneasy. Ugh, okay, that is all. My tat itches and I feel fat because I think I'm gaining weight because I'm always hungry and tired and bloated. And I think I might just go back to sleep and try to not exist. Okay, bye.

Undated

People I want to date:

–graffiti artist
–painter/someone really good at drawing
–writer/reader of great novels
–someone that wants to escape the system as much/more than me
–world traveler
–multiple linguist
–cook
–explores at night
–smokes cigs in dark alleys
–tats and piercings

It's all about you and me.

21 December 2011

So much shit has happened! We are in Amsterdam! At the International Budget Hostel. Yesterday I woke at 6:30, got ready and ate, and Kan and I packed all our shit, took some of it to storage, and went to King's Cross. We took a train to the airport because we could not find the bus we needed to take. We walked around the whole rail station and when we finally found Liverpool Street the bus or the bus stop was nowhere in sight. It was frustrating, and we had to pay £21 each for the train. Bleh.

We got through security and to our gate without any trouble at all, and we each got our own row on the plane, so we both got windows. It was only a 40-minute flight but I still took a short nap. I had a tiny pillow I took from the clothes/stuff recycle, so I was real comfortable.

When we got to Amsterdam the airport was pretty sweet. The signs were mostly in English, and we had to figure out how to get to Amsterdam Centraal, or Central Station. We took a train and we paid about four euros for it, but no one ever checked our tickets so we could have just not paid for it. Central Station is massive and beautiful. We went to the tourist office and bought a map (dumb because there are free maps everywhere), and got Kan's iPad and looked up hostels, and found the one we are now staying at.

Last night we had to sleep in different rooms, but tonight and tomorrow night we will be in the same room. Yesterday we just explored the main streets by our hostel. We also met this guy from Argentina named Edison, and we went to a "coffee shop" and bought weed, which I have the rest of right now because Edison left today.

We used a vaporizer, which I like way more than smoking. The high came on slowly and smoothly, and everything was perfect. Nirvana came on, the *MTV Unplugged* songs, so fucking beautiful. I felt like I was exactly where I was supposed to be, and so in love with Kurt, and we were together. Hahaha. But seriously. It felt like Amsterdam was just this whole new miniature world that was created just for us to play around in for a few days. So cool.

The atmosphere here is so different. It really is a whole different world than anything I've ever experienced, not just when I'm high. There are a ton of canals, alleys, bridges, bikes, cobblestones, etc. The sidewalks are kind of hard to differentiate from the bike lane and/or the road, because they are all made of the same red-brown cobblestone shit. I almost got run over like every 10 minutes. All the buildings look similar, as do the roads and canals and bridges. The buildings all look really nice and clean-cut. Like, village-like and quaint. So cool.

Today we walked all day around the whole city. We saw the Van Gogh Museum, the I Amsterdam sign/sculpture, the Old and New Churches, the Heineken Brewery, where I bought Dad a hat for his birthday, and the Red Light District. The Red Light District is so strange, it's just girls behind windows barely wearing anything. They have music and makeup and hair straighteners and curlers, or whatever they want, on this little shelf next to them. They just stand there all day, or sit on a stool or something and, like, primp. They probs get sooo bored! It's just hella creepy over there, like "live sex shows," what the fuck. That is so gross to me, but intriguing at the same time because it's so intensely foreign and unlike anything I've seen.

The whole trip has been sweet so far, but I feel like it has been tainted by Kan's fucking strange attitude. We seriously argue a lot, like about stupid shit like directions. I swear everything I say she has a snappy response to, like with a tone that says, "Obviously, you are stupid for asking that," or else she gets pissed at me for asking questions. Like, I'll ask questions but be just kind of wondering about or commenting on the specific topic, or thinking/wondering out loud, and she'll get pissed so quickly. She'll be like, "I don't know, quit asking me!" I feel like she has the shortest temper ever, and no patience at all for anything.

She gets pissed when I don't want to do the same thing she wants to do, like spend money on shit. It's just so annoying. We can't have a conversation without her acting like I'm stupid and explaining shit to me like I'm five when I already know. We haven't talked about anything real at all, like we used to. It's this weird mind-fuck situation that I keep trying to keep calm but I feel like it's not working. I try to not say anything controversial or negative or whatever, but she is still pissy. It's so motherfucking weird!

Oh, I forgot to say that last night after we did the vaporizer we went to Chipsy King! And got delicious fries with sauce. I got BBQ, and we came back to the hostel and sat in the lounge and watched these hilarious music videos, and there was this ridiculous French guy that kept asking us questions, and then he talked in French to his friend and also to

Edison, who can speak French really well and we didn't know that until he just spouted it out. Ha. It was hella tite!

I think tonight we are going to go to the Bulldog and smoke or drink. We have been sitting in the lounge for a few hours, me writing, Kan looking shit up online. I don't think I have anything else to say, other than that they play a lot of techno in the lounge and I really like it. Alright, bye!

22 December 2011

Last night Kan and I went to the Bulldog and attempted to roll a joint and it was bad. This huge black guy that was really creepy was like staring at us the whole time, and then he wanted to help us roll it, and then he offered to put tobacco in it, and I was like, "No, we don't need your help," because I am not going to take tobacco from a random stranger that is creepy. I don't care if it's just from a cigarette. I don't take chances like that, I don't ingest anything that a creepy stranger gives me. That's the first thing you learn in like kindergarten.

Kan got so pissed at me, but we didn't talk about it after we left. Then she went up to the room when we got to the hostel, and I just sat in the lounge and kept trying to roll the joint. I felt really hurt because I was super uncomfortable and anxious in the Bulldog because of that guy, and she just didn't even care, or want me to feel better. Like, if she felt super anxious somewhere and it was evident, I would be like, "Okay, where do you want to go, what do you want to do that will make you feel better?" But she was just bitchy. And I never expected that from her.

Ian was down in the lounge on the computer – we met him earlier at the hostel because he is in our room as well, and he is traveling alone. Earlier he was sitting on the couch looking super high and had a joint with him. So I asked him how to roll one, and he put some tobacco in it and rolled a perfect joint with a handmade filter. We were talking and we realized that we both went to school in London and both lived in the same dorm building at the same time. WTF! We had never seen each other before, though. He lived on the third floor apparently. Crazy.

We smoked the joint outside and walked around for a bit, and he bought some weed at a random coffee shop, and then we went back to the hostel. And to bed because we got kicked out of the lounge because it was closing. Kan was still awake when we got back to the room. Then I woke up today at 11 and everyone was gone. Kan went on a run without me and I feel hella fat. I don't know.

24 December 2011

So much has happened, holy shit. On the 22nd we took the train kind of far away to get to this electronics store so Kan could buy a charger for her camera because she forgot it. This guy John came with us and he was weird but nice. He was also in our room and in the military. I can't remember if I mentioned him already.

Then we went to Central Station to figure out my Eurail Pass, which I got for 270 euros. I think Kan's was cheaper. I had to get money out of a random ATM because they didn't take swipe debit cards, only cards with chips in them, or something. Then we walked back to the hostel and on the way bought some magic truffles, woohoo! We haven't eaten them yet. We were going to eat them while going to this botanical garden thing, but it got too late to go and have time to see everything. So we just went back to the hostel and hung out in the lounge and stuff. I read until Part II of *Atlas Shrugged* before I went to bed, and then we got up at 8:30 a.m. to get ready to check out. Then we took the train all day to Berlin, which is where we are now.

Last night we checked into our hostel, which is SO MOTHERFUCKING nice, and made friends with the people working downstairs. Finn the German and this other like Brazilian or Middle Eastern looking guy who's name I can't remember, made us drinks because it was this two-for-one deal, and they took a Jaeger shot with us, and didn't make us pay for it. Legit. We made friends with this Pablo guy from Argentina as well, and these two girls from different parts of Germany. It was so interesting talking to them.

Then we took the underground to some random stop and walked to a random club, and it was so legit. It cost €6 to get in, but it turned out to be awesome. At first there was a live band singing Christmas songs and it was kind of boring so I was just sitting on the couch. But then they started playing other music on the speakers and the band left, and Kan and I just danced awesomely. Guys would drift towards us kind of, so hilarious and kind of awkward but in a good way.

We made friends with three German guys; one just broke up with his girlfriend and was really depressed and didn't speak English very well, and we forced him to get up and dance, it was so funny. I can't remember the other one's name who was talking to Kan a lot, but he was gross, like short and stocky. The third one was named Steven and he was wearing a band shirt – The Wombats – and he bought us all Jaeger shots. And I think Heineken beers but I can't remember, ha.

We all danced on stage in front of the DJs and didn't get in trouble, and these two creepy Middle Eastern looking guys kept following us around because we smoked a joint and they wanted some, and also this like 40-year-old guy with glasses kept drifting over to me and I kept running away from him.

We finally left at around three in the morning. We got Döner kebabs at this tiny place down the street, and the people working were very nice. Then the two guys that wanted weed came in and tried to talk to us, so we left quickly after we ate. We finally got back at around four, best night ever.

Then this morning we had to check out of our room by 11 a.m. and check into another room after three. So Kan and I ate breakfast and put our stuff in the luggage room and then walked around Berlin. It was super cold so she went back early, but I explored for longer by myself and took pics with her camera.

I feel like Berlin is mostly just churches and museums and stuff, and I like it a lot. It's open and spread out and calm-ish, and misty and gray. It's quiet (I guess everything is quiet now, because I'm so used to

London's noise) but it's, like, *important*. It is a famous and significant place with a history, therefore it's safe. So I just feel safe, I dunno. It's totally a mind thing, like a certain perspective, and I could change my perspective but it's so hard.

Then when I finally couldn't handle the cold I came back to the hostel and took a nap. I dreamt that my family came to Berlin for Christmas and I was running back to the hostel to tell Kan and I kept seeing people I knew and it was so weird. And then I woke up.

Kan and I later went to Christmas Eve mass at St. Hedwig's Cathedral. So cool, all in German. It was very crowded. It ended at 11:30 p.m. and now it is 2:30 a.m. I played pool with this guy named Jobe, and I did alright. Tomorrow is Christmas! Woo. Oh, I also bought a backpack today. It's brownish, super lightweight, water resistant-ish. I dunno. I love it. And I stole a black pencil from the same store, oops.

I'm living on chocolate and oatmeal and soup. I think I'm going to go to sleep now. Blah blah blah.

26 December 2011

Yesterday was Christmas! We went to some Christmas markets, pretty sweet. Then later that night we got drunk. I drank an entire bottle of wine and talked to this British guy that is at our hostel by himself and is sexy-ish. Kan talked to her family on a payphone somewhere while I read *Atlas Shrugged* on the couch.

I also stole three croissants from the café, and then we left for the club, which we went to with some people that checked into our room yesterday: a guy named Manuel who is tall and skinny and has dark hair and eyes, and a girl named Jenny who is really skinny and has strawberry blonde hair. We met these random other people that were trying to find the club as well. It was really far from the U-Bahn station. We had to wait in line forever and I forgot my ID but they didn't card me.

We danced until like six a.m. It was the latest I've ever stayed up while partying. I left before they did because I was starving and really tired, and then I passed out in my bed and it was a beautiful moment. I made out with three guys (I think that's all), and with Kan again, ha. And we talked about how we never talked about how we made out before and it was funny. I made out with this guy that could speak German, Russian, and English, and then a German guy that couldn't speak English, like, at all, and then another guy that was kind of boring but he could speak English.

The club was super dark and there were a million people and it was like in the movies where they walk through a dark club with lights pulsing and illuminating people making out in dark corners and other dark areas. I loved it. Like, it feels meaningful and so I'm not anxious at all.

Anyway, today we slept until one or two p.m. and then we went to another Christmas market at Alexanderplatz, and I got a Nutella banana crepe, and then we went to Burger King and got fries and ice cream, and then we went to McDonald's and got cheeseburgers. And now we're back in the hostel and we just had nachos. But before the nachos I had a nap and Kan watched a movie. Tomorrow hopefully we will see the Berlin Wall and the Jewish memorial, and then take the train to Prague! So excited.

We've been getting along a lot better and I'm so happy. I think we have started to adjust and feel a lot more comfortable traveling. I love it. I could live like this forever I think. Well, I guess I will write more later!

30 December 2011

Holy shit.

31 December 2011

So much has happened I dunno where to start. Okay, I guess I'll start back in Berlin.

We did end up going to the Berlin Wall, but we didn't get to stay long because we wanted to do this free "alternative" tour. There was a little bit of the wall left but mostly it was just a ton of reddish poles standing where the wall used to run and showing how long it was. There were lots of information signs telling about the history of the wall and showing pictures from various years and different stages the wall went through.

Then we went on the alternative tour thing and learned a lot about street art in Berlin. We saw the astronaut, which is the most famous graffiti art thing in Berlin. We visited more alternative parts of the city with cool stores, and this creepy guy told me he liked me and asked if I needed weed. Haha.

The tour made us miss our train slash there wasn't a train, or something, so the train we ended up taking to Prague had a million transfers and had a five-hour or so layover in Liberec, Czech Republic, where we attempted to sleep in the train station with all these other people until we got kicked out by these 12-year-old-looking Czech security guards who couldn't speak English. HAHA our fucking lives, "What is happening to us?" We made friends with this girl from Kazakhstan and we slept until three a.m. at this hotel near the train station in the lobby with her and her parents, who couldn't speak English. It was ridiculous, in a good way.

Then we slept on the last train to Prague and it was alright. We took the underground to our hostel, the Chili Hostel. It was really cool! We talked to these British guys who turned out to be stupid and annoying, and also to this Israeli guy with longish hair named Itay. He didn't look like he was from Israel, though. We went to this sweet comic book bar and had a great Kana conversation, and later we went back to the same bar with Itay, and I totally fucked him in the men's bathroom. HA HA HA WOOHOO! It was pretty awesome.

Kan and I danced a lot onstage, and also this old guy from our hostel came with us and just sat there all night, it was hilarious. He wasn't creepy or anything, just had no friends and really liked to not stop talking. I slept in Itay's bed that night and we fucked in the hostel bed.

Haha wtf. He was a terrible kisser, though. We had to check out the next morning but were just going to a cheaper hostel. That hostel was in a safer part of Prague called New Town. Old Town is where the Chili Hostel was, or near it at least.

That night we got drunk, actually I kind of got super drunk and Kan only had one shot that I bought her. But we went to Karlovy Lázně, the club with five fucking floors. It was amazing, I cannot even describe. Each floor had its own DJ and set up. And I seriously made out with EVERYONE. It was awesome. An Australian guy with a British sounding accent that reminded me of one of the guys on the soccer team in Seattle, this 18-year-old guy that looked like he was 12, an Italian guy that wanted me to suck his dick and I was like, "No, but you can suck mine!" And then he just walked away, it was HILARIOUS! And also a few other guys that I can't really remember or describe too well because they were just generic or I didn't have a conversation with them.

We danced so much, and guys would just follow us around. Like these ridiculous Polish guys that kept showing me condoms and asking if I'd like to fuck them. Haha I was like, "Yes, I want to fuck you!" And then I ran away. And I was like best friends with the security guard outside until he let someone steal my alcohol I tried to hide. Ugh.

The next day we had to check out so we stored our stuff at the hostel and went to Old Town Square to see the astronomy clock thing and get wifi so we could figure out our Paris shit. It was really stressful because we couldn't find hostels and shit but eventually we figured it out. We took a night train without a reservation and somehow got beds! But then we had to pay 20 euros each, it was stupid. It took forever for us to find our hostel and use the underground metro but it happened.

So we took quick showers and then went to my surprise birthday event that Kan had planned, which turned out to be motherfucking CIRQUE DU SOLEIL! IN PARIS. It was so fucking legit. Then we took naps at the hostel and then went to the EIFFEL TOWER for New Year's Eve and fireworks! The tower lit up and sparkled and we took a ton of pics, so beautiful. I just cannot believe that we're actually here, it's incredible.

OMG it was hilarious, so many drunk Mexicans or just really dark guys tried talking to us at the Eiffel Tower, to the point where we eventually left because we couldn't get away from them. Everywhere we turned there were more men lurking that tried to approach us and say stuff to us. So funny but actually not funny at the same time because that is a dangerous position for a female to be in.

It took forever to get home because the metro was so crowded, but we made it before two a.m., which is when the hostel apparently locks the doors. Now it's 2:45 a.m. of 01 January 2012. I'm tired! What a perfect way to start off the new year. WOOHOO!

01 January 2012

Today we took a free tour of Paris and it was really cool. Our tour guide was an American girl living in Paris for the past year and she was very knowledgeable about the history of the city and the buildings. I learned a lot and I'm glad we did that.

After that Kan and I took a nap until seven p.m. and now she is knitting in the room and I am trying to organize my life because we leave tomorrow! Sad but it's alright.

02 January 2012

I am sitting in the café where they filmed *Amélie* waiting for a mocha. It's nine a.m. I got up early to explore Montmartre before check-out at 11. I saw Moulin Rouge as well as the place where Picasso and other artists worked and lived. Only the front of the building remains because the rest, the studios, was destroyed by a fire. This café is so cute and warm. I like it a lot. I am going to watch *Amélie* when I get back to London and settle in.

HOLY FUCK they just gave me my mocha and it's the HUGEST mocha ever hahahaha wtf it's like the biggest thing ever!!! Okay, that is all, I guess…

Except, I want to talk about Kan. Something is, like, seriously wrong. She is not the same best friend I had before and it's making me feel so fucking weird and confused. It's like everything I say she disagrees with or negates and she doesn't understand that I can feel differently and have different opinions than her. Sometimes she'll just be like, "You are stupid," or just argue with me about the smallest insignificant things, or blame shit on me.

Like, she blamed me for losing her adaptor on the train. She had asked me to unplug her charger with the adaptor connected to it because I was closer to the outlet than her. It's stupid because if I didn't unplug the adaptor with the charger, why didn't she notice that when she packed the charger, or when I handed the charger to her? She doesn't look after her own shit and then when it gets lost it's my fault. And when she gets lost and I correct her on the map, it is just normal, just whatever, not a big deal. But if I get lost she acts like I'm an idiot.

And she is always talking to me in that snappy tone and I hate it. It's so frustrating. And sad because I'm really starting to resent her presence, and I am actually excited to see her go back to Seattle, and I never in a million years thought I would feel that way. I don't know why she is so angry and irritable, and I am wondering if something is really wrong, or if it's her pills or her not taking her pills or something. Because she really is different, and…bitchy. And I don't know what to do…

The whole trip I've just tried to keep the peace and not contribute to her anger, but it's really hard because it's like my every movement fuels the fire: my every word, opinion, question. Especially questions. Which is the weirdest part because when she was little her dad wouldn't let her ask questions and it really fucked her up. And she's doing the same thing and I don't know if she knows it.

I don't know who to talk to. I will probably message Zara because she makes things better always. Or maybe Mila. I dunno. Definitely Mom. Anyway, I don't want to talk about this anymore because it's depressing.

Things: learning to not get anxious when traveling alone, spending money until it doesn't bother you anymore, knowing you'll get a job eventually because you're clever, liking schoolwork, organizing your room, getting rid of shit you don't want, excitement about getting rid of that shit, nerves about meeting relatives you don't know well, a new year, an excellent beginning to a new year, tired of figuring shit out like travel plans, hungry for something real, wanting to be able to love someone and not being able to, not having an opportunity to love someone, wanting more tattoos

04 January 2012

Ten days until my birthday. How strange. I just got on the train to Cambridge, where I will take another train to Brandon, to go to Jonah and Andrea's house! Jonah is one of my cousins on Mom's side, but he's way older than me so I don't really know him. He's in the military and is stationed somewhere close to Brandon with his wife Andrea, who I've never met. I'm going to visit them because Mom talked to her brother and his wife, who are Jonah's parents, about how I'm studying in London, and we all coordinated a time I could visit them.

I am excited to see a different part of England and also kind of nervous because I don't know them. I mean, I obviously know Jonah but the last time I saw him was probably before high school, so I don't remember how he is as a person. But I am eager to see what their lives are like and to explore Suffolk. I think it's going to be very pretty.

Yesterday I checked back into the dorms and unpacked all my shit, and it felt so good to be HOME. Kan's flight was at two but she missed it because the Piccadilly line was closed to Heathrow for some reason, so she stayed another night. We stole a ton of food from the kitchen and watched *Amélie*, and then this morning we got breakfast at Costa and parted ways. On the night of the second we used Sakura and Moe's guest passes and she slept in Sakura's room and I slept in my own bed.

Yesterday morning we went to Brick Lane and Rough Trade so she could buy a friend a birthday gift, and we also got cheap pastries at the Beigel Bake. Yum. I think that's partly why she was late, though. I think I'm glad she's gone. Which is kind of fucked up but it's true. Dunno what else.

05 January 2012

I am at Jonah and Andrea's! Their home is sooo cute and messy and family-ish. It's great. They even got me Reese's Puffs from the military base, best day EVER. Yesterday Jonah picked me up from Brandon station in his car The Punisher which is small and has flames on it and a huge stick shift with an eyeball on it, ha. So great. I met Andrea and we all hung out around the house and then went to the base to get me a visitor pass, and then to a little village type thing to go grocery shopping. I love Andrea, she is so funny and super nice.

They have a baby daughter named Maya and a dog named Patella that I'm in love with. Medium-sized, dark, scrunched up face, so CUTE. Last night we watched *Boston Legal*, *Wall-E*, and then this British comedy show that was fucking hilarious! I am going to look it up online and see if I can watch it on my laptop.

This morning I woke at like noon. Oops. I set an alarm for 10:30 but that was an epic fail. I dunno what will happen today…

Safety and security in a <u>HOME</u>

Things in life that matter: knowledge, exercise, friendship, buying only what you need or what you'll use, gifts, that family feeling, the feeling of security and that you'll be okay, reading, learning, exploring, experiencing everything, crossing off things from your lists of what to experience, yeah

I get that family, safe feeling when watching *Keeping Up with the Kardashians*, which Andrea is always watching while she works on her cooking blog.

"You have left the future" –Graffiti during train ride to Cambridge

07 January 2012

Last night I talked to Mom on the phone for an hour and it was the best thing ever! I talked about Kan and how she was different and about our travels and about school and future stuff. It was really good.

Yesterday Andrea and I went shopping and to Taco Bell on the base, it was awesome. We also visited Jonah at work, and watched a ton of *Keeping Up with the Kardashians*, which I am now addicted to, haha. I am watching it right now and taking forever to write this entry.

Tonight Jonah and Andrea are having people over for sushi and they are making it right now. I should probs be helping but I offered and they didn't give me anything to do…hmmm. I leave tomorrow but I am coming back next Thursday for Maya's birthday, and I'll be here for my birthday as well because it's the day after Maya's.

Okay, well, that's all I suppose.

I get this strange satisfaction in being able to say, "I've been there," or "I've done that."

08 January 2012

I go back to London today. We are going to drive to Cambridge and I'll take the train back to King's Cross. I am excited but I have to do a shit-ton of homework and work out, so my vacation is over. Oh well, I am glad to be busy and do schoolwork. I think.

I really have nothing to say right now. Andrea is making pasta for lunch/dinner.

09 January 2012

I just wrote Grandma the longest letter in existence. About my travels and stuff.

Today was a really good day. I had enough money on my Oyster to go to Marble Arch and back, so I went on a long run though Hyde Park, Green Park, and St. James Park. It was great. Then I dyed my hair orange on my right side and pink and red on my left side. I used up the rest of my colours, so that I only have black left, but it's that shitty black that turns to gray/blue in like two days.

I also took a huge shit today, woohoo! And I haven't overeaten either, so I feel good.

Last night I took the train back to London and I hung out with Sakura in the lounge and it was really good. I think I'm going to go to the lounge soon and work on my essays.

I slept till noon today, oops. I have been doing that lately, it's weird. I think I might take a nap right now! Woohooooo. Okay byez.

10 January 2012

Today I woke at noon again, did laundry, bought Andrea/Maya a gift, and worked out in the gym.

I have no idea why, but I have diarrhea. Now I'm scared that I have HIV or something, because getting sick is a symptom of it, and when I fucked Itay in Prague he got all worried about pregnancy and HIV when the condom broke. Why would he be worried about me getting HIV if he didn't have HIV? He kept saying, "Are you sure it's alright? I am worried about *you*." So I'm all worried about it! I messaged him on Facebook and asked if he actually has it (AWKWARD) so hopefully he won't. If he does I will get tested or some shit. God, I hate my life.

I was thinking I would so much rather have HIV than be pregnant. Which is probably stupid…no, I think I'd rather be pregnant because then I'd get an abortion. FML.

12 January 2012

Cheese, hand warmers, eye contact and shy smiles, vibrant hair, perceptions of beauty, eye makeup, television shows, a thick luster, jewelry, running, feeling so good after running, shopping for birthday gifts, getting mail, not feeling anxious for a really long time, confused by feelings of attraction, loving the attention I get from guys, loving any sort of attention, Top Ramen, lots of food, not worried about money, visiting Jonah and Andrea!

babies, puppies, coffee, ice cream, cake, alcohol, wearing clothes I haven't worn in a while, NOT being on my period, the shadow of this pen on clear white paper under dim lamplight and a darkening sky, waiting, money dripping silently from my eyes like tears of frustration I'm fine I'm totally fine just bored yet creative and not really concentrating, that guy I always see in the lounge is so fucking sexy I want his body I want him to want me, scribbles of black ink, foreign languages,

cursive, ribbons, fucking dairy products, desire to see attractive males, hemp, cannabis vodka, "oh to be drunk and escape from me," being too drunk, hangovers and how that is not enjoyable, birthday cards, showers, warmth, nothing important to say so just rambling, Nicki Minaj, being a selfish lover, *Atlas Shrugged* as a mind-blowing experience, wanting to read more, wanting to be the curves of your own letters, your own writing,

smooth sailing, graffiti as artwork and a method of communication and expression, house parties, tattoos and piercings, tolerance, big cities, never going back, wanting to go back but just to visit, wondering where you belong, wondering if you truly belong in any particular place, wondering why no one else is preoccupied with this train of thought, this idea, fucking bitches

[*Ana's birthday, 14 January 2012, begins the next profection year, activating her 9th house (again) and 10th house. 9th ruled by Libra and thus Venus, and 10th ruled by Scorpio and thus Mars. –J.]

17 January 2012

So much has happened. I spent this past weekend, including my birthday, at Jonah and Andrea's for Maya's party. I drank a ton of Sex on the Beach that they made me and ate a ton of food. All that day Andrea and I were preparing the food for the party. They got me a cute Hello Kitty mug for my birthday that I am drinking coffee out of right now, and Hello Kitty jelly beans and a Camelbak water bottle. I really needed a water bottle actually so it was perfect!

I got a ton of Facebook messages and I felt loved. I didn't go out or anything even though I turned 21, but I don't really care because I already know what it's like to go out since the drinking age here is 18 and you can go to the bars at 18.

While I was there Andrea and I planned for a trip to Paris. For next week. I am glad because I wanted to see more stuff than I was able to with Kan.

I have been back at the dorms for two days. I turned in an essay yesterday and took my Econ exam. It wasn't that bad. I finished before a ton of people so that was cool. I feel like I at least passed. Now I have two more essays due next Monday.

OMG before I went to Jonah and Andrea's for the birthday party, I got really drunk while hanging out with Sakura in the lounge. I kept making eye contact with this guy that I see in there sometimes that I think is attractive. He's foreign from I have no clue where. I was dozing on the couch kind of by where he was sitting, and I just kept staring at him and looking away and he sort of laughed, and then asked me if I wanted to go outside and smoke a cigarette with him, but I said no because I was WAY too drunk and didn't think I could walk without vomiting. Ha…And the next day he was in the lounge but I didn't talk to him. I haven't seen him since because I've been gone.

I guess that is all. Today I am going to go on a run and work on my essays…bleh. Oh wait! I totally got an awesome birthday package from Sawyer and Lacy and I am so excited and happy! Okay, that's all.

18 January 2012

Today was good. I went to the art supplies store in Brick Lane and got a new diary, razors, and a new pencil. Then I went to Daunt Books and got a Europe 2012 travel book, so excited! I also worked out in the gym. And I got a package from home with a ton of candy and a NEW DIGITAL CAMERA! OMG!! I thought they were just going to send me the red digital camera they already had, but no, I get a new one! I am so excited and happy. And I got it right before going to Paris (next week) so it's perfect!

I also made an origami ring out of a dollar bill I had, because obviously I won't use it here. I bought cigarettes today, too.

I was thinking about my life, and how I never want to stop learning and experiencing, and I feel like if I go back to Idaho I am going to forget everything I learned, like my street smarts, and how to not be awkward when talking to someone, or how to make out with guys in clubs, ha. Or just how to talk to guys I think are attractive without feeling dumb or nervous.

Idaho is so conservative and boring and there is nothing to explore or learn or experience.* The discoveries, the surprises, the mysteries, the uncovered secrets, the acting like you own the place, all of that is vibrant and eclectic and beautiful and insane. And none of that exists in Boise. But in London, in Berlin, in Paris, in EUROPE, it's everywhere.

[*Ana: The nature is nice, though, if you know where to go. –J.]

I dunno if I can live without this brilliance, even if I am in school and if I got a job as well. The diversity here, the people, the architecture, the fashion, the mini shops, even what the money looks like! And the languages! It's all so different, the whole system is so interesting to me, and for once in my life I actually want to be a part of it. I feel like instead of rejecting it, like I did for everything in Idaho/America, I am embracing it. I want to keep it and store it away for future reference.

I feel like I know how the world works! And I can't get enough of it. I need more, it's like a drug. Am I so ADD that I need to see something new, do something different, each day? Is this somehow bad? I want to know every place intimately, and once I have achieved this knowledge I want to move on, explore something new, learn about someone else's life, feel someone else's lips on my skin, see someone else's smile, have new adventures, see new scenery, try more drugs, listen to another opinion, start a fresh page, a new sharpened pencil, another book, another craft, a new door to yet another bedroom, another apartment, another life.

This impermanence fuels me, fuels my soul, my spirit, my lusts, my passions, my motivation.* This is the only thing that matters to me: learning and experiencing as much as I possibly can. And it starts NOW. It has already started, and I am so fucking lucky. I cannot believe my life is truly mine. I feel like a real person.

[*Ana: This is an excellent example of your Moon conjunct Uranus placement. How strange you are: you describe so clearly your own astrological placements without having any knowledge of astrology. Everything is hidden from you but somehow you still know, subconsciously. Maybe that's your 12th house everything. –J.]

19 January 2012

Today was good. I went on a run in the morning to Primrose Hill, which is above Regent's Park and has legit views of the city. Then I took a shower and went to Houses of Parliament and Big Ben to take pictures with my new camera. I just walked around the South Bank and looked awesome, and everybody stared. When I got back I uploaded my pics and took a long nap, and then went to the lounge and worked on my essays.

I am in the lounge now, it's 1:15 a.m. There were these German/Swedish/Norwegian guys drinking down here. I'm not sure exactly what they were, haha. But they invited me over and I got like two and a half shots of vodka from them. For free woooohoooo! Ha. They were ridiculous and not even cool, but kind of funny. I smoked a cigarette outside with them before they went to the club. Then I came back here and wrote Sawyer an email. I'll probs go to bed soon, I dunno.

I'm hoping to finish this diary before Paris next week since I got a new fucking legit one at the art store in Brick Lane. I think it would be cool to start a diary in PARIS, like what the hell!?

Oh, I forgot to mention. Last night Sakura and I met this guy named Nile, from Washington D.C., except he looks like he's from the Middle East, and he is really nice and into cool things, like headphones. He's, like, obsessed with them. He and Sakura bonded over music technology, which is what Sakura is studying, and it was awesome.

Today I also went to Primark and bought some stuff for Kan for her birthday. I bought a small bag thing to carry toiletries during my travels, and I'm going to take it to Paris. Exciting! Okay, that is all for now. Not sure what is happening tomorrow, hopefully I will finish my current essay and start my Social Problems essay. Okay bye! Love you.

20 January 2012

I am in a Café Nero on Piccadilly Street. I went in search of the White Cube Gallery, which is supposed to be right by Piccadilly Circus, but I couldn't find it, and I realized I was like faint because I don't think I ate enough for breakfast, so I decided to get a coffee at the first place I found. And it happened to be Café Nero, which is good because I used my stamp card thing, and there is an Accessorize right next to it and they had a ton of things for 70% off. I got a wallet because I've been needing one. So it worked out perfectly! Even though I didn't find the gallery.

It probably doesn't even exist, like the Photographer's Gallery, which I tried to find once and also failed. But I love when something doesn't work out but it leads to something else that is awesome, maybe even better. I guess that is all…

Tonight I am supposed to go to Taiki's "goodbye dinner" or something, but I don't want to go because you have to pay £10. Also, I think Moe is going to this Lesbian bar and I really want to go, haha. Because I have never been to a gay bar! And I wonder if girls hit on each other. Moe has to go for her hospitality class, which is part of what she is studying – stuff about hotel management I think, because gender issues are very important. Or some shit.

There is a guy in here that was writing in a large black journal, and I want to know what he was writing. I think he is attractive. I think guys that write and read in general are very attractive. Okay that is really all I have to say.

21 January 2012

Today was alright. I woke at 9:30 because I went to bed semi-early and Moe was being super loud in the morning (slamming the door, banging dishes, stomping around. You know, what she usually does).

I went on a run along Regent's Canal and it was beautiful! Such a cool place to run. I ran all the way to Camden and back, and everyone stared. There were these guys working on a boat that waved to me and smiled, and I waved back. Everyone is so nice to me, ha. Seriously, all the people smile or just stare and you can tell they think I'm interesting or attractive or whatever. It just makes me feel really good about myself.

I went to the British Library, too, and wrote like 1000 words of my Social Problems essay. It wasn't hard at all because it's just research stuff and not my opinion. Hopefully I'll be able to finish it tomorrow so I can turn it in on Monday without stressing out.

Also today I researched traveling stuff Sakura and I are going to do, and other stuff from my Europe guide book I got at Daunt Books. I want to do another Europe trip! I totally will be able to. I have to figure everything out, but I am sure it will be amazing.

I guess that's all for today. I am almost done with this diary and that is crazy. I have experienced so much in these past few months, and it's all contained in this little black book!

22 January 2012

I forgot to say that Moe and I went to Candy, this lesbian bar, for her class about hospitality, and it was so weird. I just didn't know what to do, and I felt kind of uncomfortable because I felt like girls were predators instead of safe. Because I always see guys as predators because they just want your body or to fuck you, so it was kind of strange to feel that way about girls. I don't think I liked it because girls should be safe and I didn't feel like they were and it was weird. In a bad-ish way.

Oh, and on the tube there, there was this guy listening to music with headphones and staring at me and being creepy but in a funny/good way, and we were communicating about whether other girls were attractive or not, with our eyes and nodding or shaking our heads, and it was awesome. He would blatantly check me out and I would just laugh. He got off before Moe and I, and like tilted his head, asking me to go with him, and I WANTED TO SO BADLY!! But I couldn't because I was with Moe and she would have been so confused because she was oblivious to the whole thing since him and I didn't even talk out loud.

Ugh, I was so disappointed because I actually thought he was attractive. And what a fucking crazy way to meet someone, like that legit only happens in the movies, and I want situations like that to define my life.

That is what I have dreamed of! Like, all of high school I wanted crazy shit like that to happen! And it happens, it's real and it happens to me and it's so fucking insane and I love it. I am pissed that it happened the one time I couldn't go with him. Maybe I will miraculously run into him again. Ha.

Anyway, last night I could not sleep and I ended up going to bed at six a.m. What a fucking crazy thing. So today I was tired all day and took a 2-3 hour nap and didn't work out. But I am basically done with my essay for Social Problems. It's basically bullshit.

I also went to Tower Bridge today and took pics along the water, and walked along the water for a while. I dunno, it was pretty sweet. It was sunny-ish and the clouds were cool. It wasn't a super productive/eventful day but that is alright.

I don't know what else. I am not sure if I want to start my green diary now or wait until Paris. I think I will just wait and use these graph paper sheaves until then. Tomorrow I am going to turn in my papers and go on a run, and that is all, I guess.

23 January 2012

Today all I did was turn in my papers and print shit in the library, like my hostel confirmations for when Sakura and I travel. Then I took a nap, didn't work out like I didn't yesterday, and watched YouTube videos of *Russell Howard's Good News*. I'm totally in love with him. Tomorrow I'm getting up at 7:30 to meet Andrea around 8:15 at King's Cross. For Paris! I think it will be fun.

Today so many people stared at me, more than usual, it was weird. Because I thought I looked totally nasty, but everyone was like checking me out. I think that's what it's like to be famous. I am famous, I already am.

I have been consolidating all my shit and I wrote out all my travel desires on one piece of paper, and that felt really good. I have been tired all day and I just want to pass the fuck out. Also, I am super paranoid that I'm pregnant, for no reason, so that's cool.

I am going to start my green diary and it will be a new beginning! Tomorrow, though, in Paris. With my new digital camera, woohoo! I am glad I'm going to Paris again, even though I didn't think it was that amazing, because I think Kan lost a lot of the pics from her digital camera. I want to get a pic in front of the Eiffel Tower, like the typical touristy pic.

Well I dunno what else to say, I guess that's all.

Goodbye!

CHEERS TO A NEW BEGINNING.

"Yeah, sex isn't too exciting…It isn't intellectual at all." –Kan

24 January 2012

PARIS. Tired.

26 January 2012

So much has happened. Yesterday we went to the Sacre Coeur, the basilica on the hill in Montmartre. Such amazing views. It's so beautiful; we went inside and walked around. We walked around that area on the hill, took pictures of street art we found, and got crepes.

When we were at the taxi pick-up point I tripped backwards over this porch thing and fell, it was hilarious. The guy in the store behind us was laughing. And he was also in love with me. Ha. We took a taxi to this street with a ton of shops so Andrea could buy food she was looking for.

We went to the Louvre in search of the Red Bus Tour pick-up point, and rode that around for a while. It was so cool because I got to see a ton of things I didn't get to see last time, like the Arc de Triomphe up close and the eternal flame thing. We got off at the Trocadero and I took legit night pictures of the Eiffel Tower, and we talked to the guys selling tourist stuff, and they were in love with me as well. Ha.

Then we went to dinner and it was so good; we each got an entre, main course, and dessert. And wine! So delicious. In the end it cost €104. And Andrea paid because she is so nice.

Today we are going to go inside the Louvre to see the Mona Lisa, and I am not sure what else.

28 January 2012

I am back from Paris! Thank god (haha).

Yesterday we got up early, went to the bakery by our hotel, and then took a taxi to Gare du Nord, the train station, to take the Eurostar back to London. We were in first class again, and I got a mini bottle of wine with my lunch. Awesome.

When I got back to London I took a nap and then Sakura and I went to the Big Chill House across the street and danced. And got drunk off that wine. It was awesome. But I had a hangover this morning and it sucked. I woke up around one p.m. and felt better. I dunno what I'm going to do today, probably just recover from last night…boring! I wanted to run today but I don't really feel up to it.

The day before yesterday we went to the Louvre and saw Mona; I don't really understand why she is so famous. She is nice, though. I wanted to see Jim Morrison's grave but I never got to because it closes at 5:30 p.m. and we left the hotel at like two. And it takes forever for Maya to be cooperative, and Andrea takes a while kind of, too.

But Maya was pissy the whole day, and I seriously wanted to throw her off the balcony inside the Louvre. I was so angry inside my head because we didn't get to do a lot of things because of Maya. Like go on the fucking Metro, which would have made everything *so* easy and quick!

But no, we had a stroller and a stupid baby. I seriously hate babies, and I cannot figure out why anyone would *ever* want one!*

[*Ana: Also, who the fuck would want to make someone come to this shitty plane of existence where exploitation and violence are the norm and nobody is real? –J.]

I like hanging out with Andrea and stuff, because she is never negative like Kan was, but I am starting to feel like I would rather just travel alone. Because I know how to get things done quickly and efficiently. And everyone just slows me down. Like, Andrea will state facts about stuff we see, or comment on how something will be the best way or fastest way to accomplish something, and I just know that she's wrong about it. She'll be like, "Oh, it's over here," or "We should go this way," and I'm just like (in my head), "No, I'm pretty sure it isn't that way at all." And most of the time I'm right. And it just bugs the shit out of me.

I need a travel partner that is fast-paced, street smart, up for everything, and super excited. And I haven't found that person. I guess we'll see how Sakura does as a travel companion. Hehe. I know she will be excited and want to do everything, so that is good. She always has a good attitude and I *love* that. She also doesn't want to spend money ever, so we are compatible in that respect as well.

And that's another thing about Andrea: she spends *so much* unnecessary money and it drives me crazy! Like our hotel! Not in central Paris. We could have gotten way cheaper B&B's in central Paris! Ugh. And often she drags me into stuff and I'm like (in my head), "No, I really don't want to pay for this!" But a good thing about her is that she will pay for me sometimes. Like when we go to expensive dinners, because she is obsessed with cooking and has particular restaurants already scoped out. I bet she would be way more fun to hang out with when Maya isn't there. God, I hate babies.

29 January 2012

I know who I want to be in love with: BANKSY. Or any graffiti artist. THAT is the secret revolution I've been searching for. I especially love when they don't reveal who they are to the public. That's why it's so awesome. Secret, private, darkness, explorations at night. Illegality, if that's even a word.

Today I went on a run along Regent's Canal all the way to Camden, and a bit further. It felt so good because I hadn't worked out since before Paris. Bleh.

Tomorrow Sakura and I leave for our UK adventures. First up is Newcastle. It will be exciting. I didn't really do anything else today except take a nap…I guess that is all.

Well, actually, I want to say that I think I would totally live in Berlin. Like settle down there after exploring the world. Because Berlin is so artistic and cool, and I want to learn German and have a German graffiti artist boyfriend like El Bocho.* Okay, I think that is all for reals.

[*Ana: I'm pretty sure he's from Spain. –J.]

31 January 2012

Today is our second day in Newcastle. It's so cold here! Yesterday we checked into the hostel and went exploring. We ended up at this massive shopping area with a mall, and I bought a black skirt that goes below the knees like Amelie's, for only £4! I also bought skinny brown jeans but I wore them and they stretched out and became way too big so I returned them today.

Last night we were so tired so we just passed out. This morning we had cereal and toast for breakfast; the hot breakfast wasn't free like we thought. Then we went exploring again. We went to the Baltic Centre for Contemporary Art, where I got a coffee to end my headache, and we crossed the Millennium Bridge. It's so cool and weirdly shaped and balanced.

We found the coolest teeny street filled with amazing graffiti and took a ton of pics. It was behind this bulbous, shiny building. I forgot what it was called but it was pretty neat inside. I think it was a learning center or something like that. We then took a nap at the hostel for an hour and a half, and went to an art gallery, to the shopping center, and then to Chinatown. We took a pic of the Chinese archway thing, and then had dinner/snack at this little restaurant. I just got a coffee bubble tea thing. Sakura got this rice and fish dish that she let me try. Pretty good.

And now we are back in the room. We are the only ones here, weird. Yesterday there was this Irish lady that we talked to a bit, but she left today. Also, last night we met two guys from Liverpool and their accents were so hard to understand! They were working construction jobs, I think.

Tomorrow we are going to see the university Sakura put as her second choice behind the one in London, the "Holy Jesus Hospital" (HAHA), and Highgate Street, which has cool vintage shops and a music store. Then off to Birmingham!

Today is the third day of my birth control pills where I should be having my period, but I still haven't gotten my period. I am convinced I'm pregnant, and it's freaking me out. If I am, I am going to get drunk every night to kill it. And smoke a ton of cigarettes. Hopefully it will be a miscarriage. Ha, this sounds bad. But I seriously think I would do that. Or just get an abortion. I wonder how much those cost…If I got one I would tell Sakura but no one else. It would be a secret because I don't have that many terrible secrets and I feel like everyone else does.

I feel like I was always too anxious to allow stuff to happen. Too anxious to do anything bad, so this would be a start of my fucked up life of real-ness. Hmm. I dunno how I feel about that. I don't have morning sickness or anything so hopefully I'm not pregnant. Ugh. Lame.

01 February 2012

On the train to Birmingham. I got my period last night! Muahaha best thing ever.

This morning we went to some vintage shops and a sweet music store where we bought old *NME* newspapers about Kurt! I got the one that was printed when he killed himself. Crazy.

I have been sleeping on the train and I don't know why I am so tired because I got a lot of sleep last night. I have been in an irritable mood because of my period.

Things that are irritating me:

1. The sun shining in my face.

2. Sakura: apologizing for everything she does, talking all the time, sharing my food because she doesn't buy her own, freaking out about buying train tickets and sleeping in a hostel with guys, feeling embarrassed by everything like buttoning her jacket wrong when NO ONE would ever notice.

3. Feeling bloated because of my period and wanting to eat all the time.

4. The train jolting when I'm trying to write.

I haven't been feeling amazing mentally. Sakura's been getting on my nerves because she follows me around and I really need space, especially when I'm tired and irritable and on my period. And I just needed alone time. So right now she is in the hostel room, I think, and I am in the lounge. I tried to take a nap but I was too anxious and real cold, so I made some tea and I kind of feel better.

I just am in the weirdest mood, like I don't want to talk to anyone and I feel uneasy, like not safe. Like the typical anxiety about having a job and taking care of myself. It's fucking stupid. It's money, it's the system, it's wondering if I need to meet everyone in the hostels, everyone that looks slightly interesting, because maybe I could learn something from them. I get sort of jealous and feel that they are better than me or more experienced, and then I get depressed. Or feel intimidated, and feel anxious meeting people.

I feel like this is only happening because of my period. Also, I don't feel that amazing because I've only been eating crumpets all day and haven't had like a legit meal. So that is what is happening right now. I feel weird but am starting to feel better. I feel really indecisive right now. And it is not fun. UGH.

02 February 2012

Today we explored Birmingham and it's pretty cool. I think I like it better than Newcastle, probably because it's bigger and seems more diverse. I have seen a ton of interesting people. I found *Heavier Than Heaven*, Kurt's bio, at this used bookstore for only two pounds! So exciting! I have been looking for it for so long.

Sakura and I took, like, a four-hour nap. Kind of ridiculous. Now we are trying to buy train tickets online in the lounge by the fire.

Yesterday I didn't feel that great, but I feel better today. Last night we took hot showers, and it was seriously the best moment of my life. Our building isn't really heated, so it's super cold. Our room is warmer but not that much. We leave tomorrow for Brighton!

Good things: sitting by the fire, hot tea, fire as the only light in the room, dulled voices and conversation, TV shows. It all makes me feel safe and at home.

What may be a cause of my anxiety is not knowing how to survive in the wilderness alone. True or false?

What right do we have to live comfortably and safely, pleasurably and without pain? What right do I have to be safe from harm while others live in danger? Do I deserve this? Do I deserve to be okay?

06 February 2012

I am in my first class of the semester! A psych class, so excited.

We got back to London yesterday and I just organized my life. I did laundry and washed my dishes and worked out and it felt very nice.

Brighton was so beautiful. It was absolutely freezing but it was sunny-ish on the day we walked along the beach. The sea was so light, like a pale green, lovely. We went to the pier and took a ton of pictures and watched people playing arcade games inside and riding the rides outside, which I would like to do sometime when it gets warmer.

We also went to a lot of shops and stores along busy streets, and I bought a bag for 10 pounds that fits both my Polaroid and fisheye cameras in! It's so perfect, and I had been looking for something like it for a while now. Woo.

I am back at the dorms now. I couldn't finish writing in class because Katie, this girl on my floor, sat close to me and also class started. It's not quite dark but the moon is radiant and almost full. I have to go back to the same classroom at six p.m. because a guest speaker is going to talk about something concerning psychology. How exciting! That was not sarcasm; I really am looking forward to it.

Today I have been collaging and listening to music. Moe had class at two p.m. so she hasn't been here, and it's nice to be alone because she is ALWAYS in here; she literally will not go outside the room unless she needs something from the kitchen. It's insane to me. She is on the computer all day. I would get so bored and antsy and need fresh air! Weird.

I feel bloated even though I am done with my period and haven't severely stuffed myself. This weekend I am going to Jonah and Andrea's. I think it will be fun. Andrea said we are going to go to tea and I think that will be cool because I haven't gone to an authentic British tea house yet, and I think it's something I should do if I'm living in Britain.

It's 5:15 p.m. I think I will leave in about 15 minutes. Well I guess that is all, I will write more later!

08 February 2012

I am currently waiting inside the Barclays by King's Cross to open an account so I can cash my check from the university for doing the audit job.

Yesterday I went on a super long run along the canal and it felt amazing. Sunny, cold, clear. Beautiful. I watched *28 Weeks Later* and made collages. Now I'm in my second class! Aesthetics and Visual Culture, going to be fucking awesome, I expect. I made my Barclays account and went back to the dorm and slept for an hour, then bought cheese at Iceland, and then came here.

Oh, I wanted to say that watching *28 Weeks Later* was sweet because it was filmed in London and I saw all these places that I've been to. It's the best feeling ever to be able to say that I live there when I see something in a *movie*. Especially such an incredible movie…with zombies.

Anyway, last night Sakura and I drank and then wanted to go to the Rocket, but we took the tube to Euston Square and it ended up being so far away! So we walked all the way there and then it turned out to be closed because it was after midnight. So we just walked all the way back to King's Cross. It was so fucking cold.

We met these three guys on the walk back and they wanted to go to Fabric but I didn't go. I kind of ditched them by walking really fast and going to my room, so I'm not sure if Sakura went with them or not. I don't think she did. Well anyway, I must go because class has started!

Undated

Being able to say "I've seen that in person" or "I live there" – it's the most glorious feeling, it's liberation at its finest, it's a revolution, an escape, justice, pride, the feeling of being somewhere where important things happen, opportunity, variety, fertile ground for creativity, life?

13 February 2012

TO BANKSY:

I want everything that's in your mind, I need a revolution, I need something secret and important to give me a purpose, to show me life means something more than surviving. I want it to be mine and only mine, I want to cradle my purpose under the darkness in a back alley. I want to escape the social values.

How can you do anything if you think everything is pointless, futile? There is a rush in giving a message to the world, there is a rush in giving a message to you, I don't know you, maybe I am you, maybe there is a small part of you in everyone. I don't want to be anyone. I want to be separate from everyone else but a part of something big. Have you escaped the slavery of money and society? Have you escaped the system?

Where are you? How can I find you? I see you everywhere but you slip away under black paint and words I want to say. Why isn't your art on the building where I live? Why isn't your art by King's Cross? I can't find it anymore, it's too secret. I want in on the secret.

Do you get a lot of mail? Are you still alive? When you wake in the morning do you fully realize the impact you've made on the world? Do you feel the same as you've always felt? Are you afraid your mask will come off? Will you ever read these words? Do you feel that other people's poetry is painfully boring?

I love this catharsis, will you keep it a secret? Send me a telepathic message. I don't want to be the same as anyone else, I can't stand the mindless eyes of worker bees. I want art, I want rebellion, I want no anxiety about earning money to eat. Why do I have to eat? Why do I have to sleep? When do you sleep? How old are you? What do you want? Have you always wanted this?

Is there safety in a world such as this? What are you doing *right now*? Are you writing a book? Are you creating something new? Are you deciding what you'll wear today? Will you ever stop creating street art?

This is an unedited first draft. This is my original train of thought. This is subjective reality encased in language. Do you ask enough questions? If you could live your life over again would you do anything differently? If you could have another talent what would it be? Do song lyrics inspire you? Do you make lists? How do you decide where to put your art? Do you like Hello Kitty?

Truth is, I'm in love with you. I'm in love with the fact that I don't know who you are. I'm in love with the mystery, the signs of your existence, but no face to put to your name. I'm in love with your mind and the things you write. I can't love anyone I know because no one is good enough, artistic enough, intelligent enough. No one encompasses the revolution I desire. I can only love famous people or dead people or characters in books that were never real.

I love you because I know I'll never meet you. I'm in love with black paint and the images it forms. I'm in love with the excitement when I come across your work inadvertently and pretend I'm part of the secret, pretend I helped or saw you creating from afar. I love you because the world revolving around you is a mystery I can't quite reach.

–Ana

p.s. I just wanted to tell you these things because I would want to know if someone felt this way about me and the things my mind is capable of.

15 February 2012

Atlas Shrugged encompasses the secret revolution I've always yearned for.

17 February 2012

I have been putting off writing in here for so fucking long, holy shit. Today is Friday, done with the first two weeks of the second semester of school. I love all my new classes. I created a Barclays account and got all that shit set up. I went on a run along the canal to Camden today and yesterday. I think it's starting to stay lighter outside longer, and I'm so glad.

Valentine's Day was super lame, as usual. The day after, however, was awesome. The dorms had a karaoke night and Sakura and I got super drunk and sang! We sang by ourselves, ha. I sang "Teenage Dirtbag" – best song ever. She sang "Down." And Moe sang too but I missed it because I was going to the bathroom.

Today Sakura and I are going to get drunk and go to the Big Chill House. Dancing! Hopefully it will be fun. I feel like I have nothing else to say, which is weird because I haven't written in so long it seems like.

The dorm security guard named Nadeem is in love with me, and I figured out how to do the cat eye makeup thing. Okay, well, I guess that is all. I am going to go mix vodka and rosé wine together because I'm insane.

18 February 2012

Last night was fucking crazy. Sakura and I pregamed in the lounge with Ashley and Brian, these two people we met at the karaoke thing, and we all went to the Big Chill House. Moe went too but she left super early. Sakura left early as well because it was too loud for her. Brian and Ashley followed me around the whole time, *especially* Brian. I know he is attracted to me and I feel bad because I think he is gross. But he seriously kept following me and it was so annoying.

Eventually I hooked up with this Greek guy, or Albanian or something, and we were making out and grinding and then we were making out on the couch and his friend was taking pictures. I could totes see Brian out of the corner of my eye, like, watching me when I first kissed the Greek guy, and that was the last I saw of him and Ashley…oops. I kind of ditched them but I feel like I don't have to babysit them. They are perfectly capable of doing their own thing.

Anyway, I went to the Greek guy's house, which was actually his friend's one room apartment, so we fucked in the kitchen on the floor, ha. And I have the worst hickey in the history of hickeys, but I put a shit-ton of makeup on it and it's like almost under my chin/jaw so it's not too blatant. But holy shit.

He had to get up at five a.m. to go to work – CONSTRUCTION work hahahahaha! And then at like six I woke up to his friend grabbing my boobs, trying to force me to hook up with him and it was scary, kind of, and I was like STOP! This isn't funny, you are scaring me! And then he had to go to work at like 6:15 or something so I left as well. He wouldn't give me a jacket or anything because I didn't have one. He was stupid. I was like, can I borrow a jacket? And he said no, or like that he didn't have one or something, and I was like OMG asshole.

The guy I had sex with was so cute and nice. We added each other on Facebook, mainly because his stupid friend demanded it. Ew, and then he jacked off after I was like NO. He went back over to his couch. Ew. Thankfully the bus stop was right by their house and it came quickly. But I got off at like Chapel Market, so I had to walk all the way back to the dorms from there. I ran part of the way to warm up. It sucked.

I'm so glad I got home super early though, because it wasn't really a walk of shame. I just looked like a fucking prostitute. God.

Today I have been organizing, collaging, and I also did laundry. Moe is at the British Library so I'm listening to music. I love when she is gone. It's raining so I am staying inside. I guess that's all…Jesus, my fucking life. My nightlife adventures.* Fuckin' hell.

[*Ana: That was insanely fucking reckless of you, and you ended up getting sexually assaulted. That night the Moon was conjunct Pluto on your Moon in the 12th Capricorn, all squaring Venus in your 3rd Aries. The Sun was conjunct Neptune, both widely conjunct Chiron and

Mercury. If he did in fact assault you at 6 a.m., the AC would have been at 26° Capricorn, conjunct your Sun-Saturn-North Node conjunction, ruler Saturn retrograde in Libra squaring it all. The Moon at that point was at 14° Capricorn, conjunct your Neptune, both trining Mars retrograde in Virgo. –J.]

20 February 2012

Yesterday Sakura and I got up early to do a *Harry Potter* tour, but we weren't able to because we didn't book an exact date in advance. So instead we walked all over London, it was awesome. We walked by Piccadilly, along Regent Street, through SOHO, to Oxford Circus and past that until Regent's Park. It was crazy. It was nice, though, because it was super sunny!

When we got back to the dorms I took a nap from like 2:40 to seven. OOPS. And oh, I forgot to say we went to this sweet hidden vintage store and I bought the coolest dress ever. It's red with small black stripes, tight, short, and has ruffles around the waist that totally hide my love handles. It's fuckin' awesome.

Also, Nikos, the guy I went home with the other night, kept calling me, and he texted me and wants to hang out again. I kind of want to hang out with him only because he doesn't speak English and I can boss him around or something. And make him buy me shit. Ha. He is so cute.

22 February 2012

Things: I can't love anyone. I can't enjoy physicality, all I want is to not touch anyone, to sleep alone, to sit in the shower and be silent and feel the warmth mixing with my own mind and my secret ideas and thoughts. All these guys want to get with me but it's not fun for me because they don't understand my mind, they don't get it, and I need that most. I'm only physical when I'm drunk and I don't give a shit about those guys, they aren't real people to me, they have no mind, no emotion, no feeling.

They are simply beings of desire, animals searching for pleasure, for a warm body to remind them they're alive. It's pitiful, it's pathetic, it's futile.

I need someone with ideas, with revolutionary thoughts, with creative urges, with plans of adventure. I need an intellectual, I need someone who reads, who researches, who *doesn't need me*. I need someone who has too many things in his head, who pretends he doesn't feel anything for me.

I need someone with infinite patience, I need someone to not touch me until I want to be touched. I need someone crazy, I need someone insane.

Where are you?

Where are you?

I want a troubled mind, I want violent urges, I want hurt and fear and worry and psychology. I want philosophy. I hate the happy-go-lucky person. I cannot stand him.

Alright. Yesterday I went on a walk along the South Bank to calm my nerves, because the day before (after class) I was so anxious all day, about jobs and CVs and living under bridges. So I walked, took pictures, and listened to music and it was all very nice.

Then this Middle Eastern guy who was kind of attractive stopped me and was like, "Do you want company?" And I was like, "Sure," and we went to coffee and he was obviously in love with me, and we walked all over London and got McDonald's, and exchanged mobile numbers, and then I was like, "Okay, I have to go." He was so clingy and needy and touchy. I told him he was, ha. And he had to look up some of those words in his dictionary translator thing on his phone. Hilarious.

I don't understand why guys are so fucking needy all the time. It's annoying.

After I got home I took a shower and Sakura and I hung out in the lounge. I figured out a ton of our spring break travel stuff, and today I want to go ask the Eurostar people a couple questions.

I dunno what else. I want to not be angry/frustrated/anxious today. I'm starting my period in like a week. Bleh.

26 February 2012

I am so annoyed at myself for not writing more frequently. I just haven't felt like it at all lately, I dunno why.

Anyway, on Friday night I hung out with that guy I met along the South Bank, his name is Soran. We went to Brick Lane and drank at a club right by the Big Chill Bar. It was cool, really big and spacious, but it closed at midnight, which sucked. He bought me five shots haha, AND I didn't even get that drunk, isn't that weird? I think I am building a tolerance for alcohol and that really annoys me.

Well, we ended up getting a hotel…haha. It was £110 and he paid. Isn't that fucking ridiculous? OMG. And then he had to work the next morning and I walked around London in the sun along the Thames for a while before going back to the dorms. I went on a run and just hung out for the rest of the day. Today I went on a run and got groceries and now I feel like falling asleep but I know I shouldn't. It's been sunny all week.

I don't really want to see Soran again because I'm not in love with him at all and he's so fucking clingy. He called me twice yesterday and once today, and texted me yesterday, too.

I think I have started to feel bored. Or maybe it's just this week. I've started feeling anxious about money again, but I try to ignore it. I watched the whole first season of *American Horror Story* and it's the best ever.

I don't know what else. My life is just ennui. Seriously. Everything bores me in the end. People, especially. Nothing's good enough.

27 February 2012

Good vibrations: a clean sheet of paper. That's all.

Things: sickness, jealousy that people can speak more than one language, chronic boredom, wanting to eat everything, feeling bloated and gross, not talking to anyone, being alone, not wanting to deal with resumes and applying to jobs, feeling that every person is boring, finding men to be annoying as fuck and immensely predictable, not being understood, no one trying to understand, repulsion, disgust, irritation, ennui, being angry with Kan because our Europe travels consisted of her being bitchy the whole time and now she acts like it was normal or didn't happen that way and we can go back to being best friends.

And that really hurt me, her attitude during our travels. I didn't want to be around her anymore. And I don't want to now.

29 February 2012

I think today will be a good day. At least I hope so. I finally started my period – got me kind of worried for a while there…I have been feeling bloated and wanting to eat everything…I am sick, too. Yesterday I bought cough drops and ibuprofen, and Mom Skyped me! It was cool.

Lately I have been obsessed with *Atlas Shrugged* because I calculated it out and found that if I read seven pages a day I'll finish before spring break. So that is my goal. And I have totally been reading more than seven pages a day.

Anyway, everything in that book makes so much sense to me. Like her ideas about love and uniting the mind and the body, and about the purpose of existence. It just feels so right to me. And I seriously hate people that think Ayn Rand is stupid. It just does not make sense to me at all, because she is so obviously a fucking genius. It's just so incredibly apparent, how can one miss that?

Oh, people have started contacting me on Couchsurfing! I posted an open request/travel itinerary thing for our spring break travels, so people can see if they want to host us instead of me contacting people first. They are like, we want to host you, or we might be able to host you but we aren't sure yet. It's so fucking cool because I didn't email them first. Awesome.

I dunno what else to say. I have class at two. We are going to talk about Kant and I think it will be interesting. I'm not sure if I already told you, but this weekend Sakura and I are going to visit Andrea. Yesterday we went to the Japan Centre by Piccadilly to get groceries for Andrea because she's going to make us Japanese food. Legit. Well, I guess that is all.

DRUNK: It's like you're so completely aware that what other people think is entirely irrelevant.

01 March 2012

South Bank. Sunny, warm. All I need is a sweatshirt. I hung out at the skate park and watched these guys do graffiti and played with their dogs. Then a homeless guy came and talked to me for a while, his name was Jamie. He was pretty nice. Not many teeth. Had walked all the way from Birmingham. That is sooo fucking far.

There is a sunny haze over the city. The buildings are pointy grayish silhouettes against a soft fuzziness of yellow and white. It's weird hanging out in London outside. I cannot believe this is my life. It feels like I'm going to get back to the States and feel like London never happened.* I dunno. It's just strange that these places exist and that I exist and get to visit them. I dunno.

[*Ana: Yeah. –J.]

Undated

Not feeling like a real person, not having any goals or direction, no strong desire to do any particular thing, not feeling I've deserved the things I'm given because I haven't earned it or worked hard for it, but at the same time having no desire to work hard for something – nothing seems worth my hard work and effort. I feel like I don't have the *right* to do anything I want to do, like artistic things, because I didn't go to school for it or study it. And I feel like I would be cheating…

"THE RIGHT TO DO SOMETHING" – does everyone have the right? If not, how do you know you have it?

WORDS OF ENCOURAGEMENT:

Everything is going to be alright, other people are in the same boat as you, some are worse off than you.

Everyone feels like they're not good enough. It's not just you.

Don't be afraid to talk about anything. You shouldn't be afraid of reality.

You will always succeed in trying.

We are all crazy. Every person you read about in the history books had some kind of "disorder," they just knew how to use it.

Don't take anything too seriously.

There is NO wrong or right way! You can do whatever you want to do.

05 March 2012

I am back from Jonah and Andrea's and I have so much food. Sakura came too and we went to the commissary and freaked on our leashes. It was fun. Sakura drives me crazy but it's okay. I try to be nice.

I have been so fucking paranoid that I'm pregnant. I did get my period this month, it ended yesterday, but it was three days late and super light. And I read online that you can still be pregnant if you get what appears to be a super light period, because it's not actually a "period." It's like vaginal bleeding or something to do with the embryo implanting in the uterus.* I don't know. I am just way overanalyzing and freaking myself out.

[*Ana: You're talking about "spotting." Blood when you wipe but not on your underwear. You are terrified of the unknown. –J.]

I drank half a bottle of wine last night so hopefully I'll have a miscarriage if I am prego. I just feel like I am because I think the woman fat on my stomach (under my belly button) is larger.* And I'm crazy.

[*Ana: You're gaining weight and feel like shit all the time because you eat terribly and drink way too much alcohol. Eat vegetables, cook things, and stop eating animal products, fast food, and a fuck ton of sugar. Or at least eat way less of those things than you do. Don't count your calories and don't weigh yourself, because that shit doesn't even matter. Just don't eat garbage and you will begin to see the difference! –J.]

Anyway, on the train to Brandon I finished John Galt's 55-page-long speech! It only took me two days to read and it went by way faster than I expected. I loved it! I am going to try to finish *Atlas Shrugged* this week.

Oh, I skipped class today because my alarm never went off! Seriously, it wasn't just me turning it off in my sleep, it really never went off. God, that is so fucking annoying to me. And then I checked to see if it works by setting it for one minute later than the current time, and it worked. GOD.

The two guys that have been texting and calling me all the time have stopped over the weekend. Thank god. I am sick and felt shitty this morning, but took a nap after breakfast and feel okay-ish now. I don't know what to do today because I kind of feel like shit and don't want to walk all day long. I dunno.

Moe just left for school WOOHOO! So I am in my room alone and it feels so nice. Maybe I will stay here and have some quiet time…and read? Oh, I forgot to say I bought a Holga camera online for like 30 pounds. It hasn't arrived yet, but I am excited! My fisheye has been annoying me because it has no flash, and this Holga has four different colors of flash, FOUR – do you hear me!? How fucking awesome is that!

I am going to name it Kyoko because that is Maya's middle name and I love it. Okay, I think that is all for now.

10 March 2012

I'm drunk, alone, and watching *Harry Potter*. The seventh, Part I, to be exact. It feels so good. Today I was ANGRY. I went to Brick Lane to take pictures with my new Holga and this guy started talking to me, and he was nice and all but I just wanted to be alone. I have been thinking about so many things and I feel like since I am drunk right now they are somehow irrelevant. But I think that in reality they are important.

1. I cannot deal with men lately. (Or I just want to be alone.) Why is it that when I want to be alone all the people talk to me, and look at me? I feel as if I'm famous and I have to hide. It's so motherfucking annoying. I'm sick of Middle Eastern-ish guys checking me out. I'm sick of people. I don't want to exist. Being drunk and watching *HP* feels so safe. I guess that's all for now. I don't know…

What's happening to me? There is so much more to say, but I'll tell you when I am more sober…At least I'll try. :D?

11 March 2012

I am in a Café Nero right next to the Golden Hinde Galleon Ship, which is some ridiculous tourist thing. I'm in the South Bank. Today there was filming or something going on and parts of London were closed off. In between the Thames and the Strand. It's sunny and warm today! Awesome. Oh, today is also daylight savings, but now that I think about it I am wondering if that's only in the US and London is at a later date. Because London changed during the fall before the States did…dunno.

Anyway, I am sort of jittery because I was like starving and had smoked a couple of cigarettes and…yeah. My handwriting isn't too beautiful right now. But at least it's better than last night's drunken scrawl. Hahaha.

I bought a mozzarella, tomato, pesto Panini. Toasted. Fucking delicious.

It's so pretty out. I love the sound of the water slapping against the walls when I walk along the bank. I dunno what else.

Yesterday I really was so angry! So I bought alcohol and got drunk alone. And it felt so incredibly good. Because I have this terrible case of ennui and I need an adventure, a cause, a purpose, something so important that I can give my attention to. Watching *Harry Potter* fills the void because they have a mission. And also being drunk makes me happier, or more excited about shit, or makes shit more real. Ha, I dunno.

Okay, well, I guess I'm going to go, I don't have anything else to say. I probs do, actually, but I can't remember right now.

16 March 2012

Today is Friday. I had a pointless Research Methods seminar and skipped my Health Psych class and slept instead. I watched a ton of Russell Howard and I am in love with him and depressed because I don't have him or anything like him.

Last night was the dorm talent show and Sakura and I got drunk and it was awesome. Because the SAME guys were hosting that hosted at karaoke! And we hung out with them at the end and I kissed the tall one, Alex. Alex and James. They were cool. And Alex got my number but I don't know if he will even text me. I don't know if I want him to text me.

I just feel like getting to know people is so hard, because it feels futile to me because they'll never know everything I want to say, or think, or feel. I feel like it would take ages for them to know those things and I don't want to try. It just makes me feel alone. More alone than when I am literally alone. Because no one gets it. And I feel like I would be awkward if I met Alex again but sober. Because, I dunno. I just wouldn't know what to say. It's stupid.

Alex was actually cool, though. I can't remember everything because I was drunk, but he was wearing a *Trainspotting* t-shirt and said he was studying Psychology. Initially I thought James was attractive. He has really nice arms. I helped them bring out the equipment to Alex's car and I am pretty sure James called me the sexy helper or something.
Haha. WTF.

Oh, yesterday I also went on a run around Regent's Park and up Primrose Hill. It felt so good. It was sunny and warmish! And there were lots of people to look at. It was good because I rested in the grass for a while and everything was calm and there was a breeze and it was so beautiful to be able to be alone and quiet.

I think I am starting to get sick of London. I miss the US. Not Idaho, but America.*

[*Ana: Lol, "America." The Stolen Land. –J.]

Undated

FACTORS:

–mental disorders
–how long it takes me to adjust to new environments
–do employers actually think that CVs accurately reflect that person? It's only a trim and tailored idealization, essentially a lie. Everyone is doing the same thing; everyone uses the same words they think will make them sound good. It's stupid, it's bullshit.

Characteristics:

–polite unless injustice
–introverted —> energy obtained from quiet/alone time (refuel)

19 March 2012

THINGS: Who cares? About anything? How do you care? Futility.

How are we to survive? How can I conquer my own irrationality? Slight changes in my mind – hopelessness/despair, then excitement for the future; feelings of doom and that bad things are happening, and then the feeling of opportunity.

HOME means: a printer, clothes I haven't worn in forever, legit alone time (no Moe), bigger living space, selling clothes, applying for jobs, real classes, real homework, family, spending less money, downloading music?, watching TV, being in an actual HOME, not just a place to live, working on my book?, real food, forward in time, organization, DIY, crafts,

London means: exploration, artistic things, riding the tube and the buses, interesting people, water, travel, going home with guys, partying, no curfew, no checking in with parents, trains, independence, new things every day, *Russell Howard's Good News*, liberal, unconventional, crazy, unique, REAL people,

Undated

fragile, sloppy, decomposing, using the correct tenses, wind and sun, stuff, stuff, stuff, stuff, the coming of the end, the warmth of the sun on only one side of your face,

25 March 2012

Zack de la Rocha, wine, bloated (blotation?), worry all the time, confusion about what I am supposed to be doing, anger, ANGER, tired, wanting to cry when someone smiles at me, no friends, feeling like I can't deal with living, being anxious, being GUILTY of nothing and everything, wanting to be obliterated,

GUILT: deserved or undeserved?

Should I be happy that I'm fucked up? Because I'm glorified, somehow I'm glorified. I feel that it won't be okay but it will! It will be okay. Wine makes it better, Mom makes it better, I make it worse, when boys look at me it makes it better but sometimes worse, sometimes I want to kill.

Do we have the right to live in luxury? What is it about humankind that I feel is low, that I feel does not deserve what it has somehow obtained?

How can I know that I'm safe? How can I possibly know this!?!?!?!

how how how how how how

Seriously, just relax, you drive me fucking crazy, just talk with ease.

Nothing else to say! Only the feeling of the [illegible] of the [illegible]

27 March 2012

Whoa, many days since I last wrote. What have I been doing? Sakura and I finally went on the *Harry Potter* tour, it was pretty sweet.

I have been quite anxious lately. About money, about life, about not having any friends. I just feel like I'm going to die, ALL the time. And everything is hostile, threatening. And I feel guilty, for spending my parents' money, for not talking to people when I think they are interesting. I judge people too quickly, I don't like anyone but I forget that people are complicated.

I don't trust anyone, especially men. I don't see men as having thoughts about anything other than sex. They don't have intelligence, they don't have respect.

I don't know how to be involved without talking to people and being anxious. It doesn't work, you always have to talk to people. I don't have friends. I need a guy friend that I can look up to and be in love with, without him being attracted to me.* I want to be the one in love. I want them to know I'm in love with them but not let me know they know. I want to try and hide it.

[*Ana: Saturn – the teacher, the guru, the mentor, the "wise, old". You were in love with him before you knew him as the master of your nativity, your personal demon and lover and vice and guide, the lord of your ascendant. The lord with many guests. Maybe he is what Jung would call your animus. You belong to him. Let go of expectations. –J. 10.15.20, 23:10, Mantua, UT]

Would people consider me lonely? Do I consider myself to be lonely?

I'm going to write a few books. The first will be *Musings*, the second will be *Letters to People I Don't Know*, and the third will be *Lists*. Or I might call the third *Lists of Vibes*. Don't know yet; still have to figure that out.

Today I slept till 1:30 p.m., whoops. And I was anxious and worrying about how we are going to get to Belgium. I think we are going to fly instead of taking the Eurostar because it will be cheaper. I think. Ugh I don't know. I still have to figure it out. Bleh.

Right now I'm sitting outside in the sun along Regent's Canal. It's nice. I brought my sketchbook and have been painting.

I think I've calmed down a bit, but I still feel bad. I mean, I just feel so afraid. Fuck, I don't know. I just don't feel safe and I don't know what to do for fun. I don't know what is fun for me. I don't think anything is fun. I want to hang out with Sawyer because he is safe. He is so safe because we feel the same things* and it's okay. Because he is figuring out his life and it gives me hope. Even though I think hope is a stupid concept…

I need a job where it's quiet, where I can do what I need to do and refuel my mind.

[*Ana: But do you, though? –J.]

29 March 2012

A letter to Damon Albarn:

Hi. How are you? I miss you. I miss you and I don't even know you. I miss you because I saw you only once at your concert in Seattle. I cried the whole time.

Everything you say is serious and beautiful and poetic and romantic. Romantic in a way that is different, more special, secret and thoughtful and like looking up to someone. Not sexual, it doesn't have to be sexual. The way Noodle is small and talented and respected and does her own thing and the only girl in the group. Like a precocious younger sibling you'd protect with your life.

You know, I've always wanted to be Noodle. Because she contributes to the group, she works, she knows what she's doing, and at the same time she's protected, she's safe, she's not alone in a shit world that's boring and fearful. She is part of something but can wander off alone and be okay.

I wonder, do you get a lot of fan mail? What do you do when you are alone? Do you ever talk out loud to yourself when you're looking in the mirror? Is there someone you really admire? In the way I admire you? You know, of course I am in love with you, but it's in that older sibling way. That feeling when you're younger that your older sibling is the most amazing person, awe-inspiring? It's along those lines. I think that's the only way I'll ever love anyone. Sexual things bore me.

Anyway, I love you because of your lyrics. I love you because Gorillaz always makes me feel better. Always. Because your music is so… Quality. The emotions are real, palpable. There's a story and somehow I'm always in it. Sometimes I'm the main character. Sometimes I'm in the background, or Noodle playing her guitar on the floating island, alone. Lost in thought, nature, subtle vibrations, a slight breeze.

I'm in love with you because you are 2D and I'm in love with 2D. I love you because you don't care about money. Because you represent things I wish I could be, that I feel I could be one day. Because your music reads my mind, because I pretend it's only for me, it was made for me and no other.

01 April 2012

In Brussels! We took the Eurostar here yesterday. Took the train to De Bruckere station, walked to the check-in place, which is not the same place as the hostel for some reason, and then backtracked to get to the actual hostel, which is like 15 feet away from Grand Place, which is fucking Grand! It's this open square with huge sweet buildings, old and intricate architecture. We couldn't find the hostel at first because it's like hidden: a tiny paper sign in the window and that's it.

But once we did find it we settled in and found a café to eat dinner. Cute place, with a really cute French guy, haha. I got a croissant with cheese and a hot chocolate and Sakura got an omelet. Yum. Then we went back to the hostel and talked to Cyrus and Henry who were drinking. They were funny. Studying in England and 17 and 18. Young. Cyrus talked a lot and was ridiculous. After they left four other guys came, studying in Germany but all from the US. Conor was hilarious because he is so obviously gay and reminded me a bit of River from high school lololol. They were nice…went out drinking. Then Sakura and I went to sleep!

And now I am drinking coffee – the only breakfast they offer – and Sakura is taking a shower. It's 10 a.m. and we are going to walk all over Brussels today and see everything ever. I am in a good mood! Excited and un-anxious. Sometimes I get small flashes of anxiety about money and such, but they go away really quickly. It's good.

Yesterday before we left I Skyped Mom for a while and it was really good. We could seriously talk for ages. Which I think is healthy.

I feel like a world traveler. I seriously know how the world works, and I know how to get myself from one place to another. It makes me feel very accomplished.

Well, I suppose that is all, I might go get dressed now or something…

03 April 2012

On the way to Hamburg.

The second night in Brussels was awesome. We got drunk with Cyrus and Henry and talked to this ridiculous Brazilian guy. That day Sakura and I walked all over the city and saw everything we wanted to see. And took a ton of pictures. I slept in Cyrus' bed, and we basically had a threesome with Henry.* Sakura went to bed early…It was awesome. But they updated my Facebook status saying I wanted to sleep with the Brazilian guy. Henry updated while Cyrus held me down, ha. Not cool.

[*Ana: I feel like this is an exaggeration but I can't really remember. –J.]

The next morning we had to check out and it sucked because we were hungover. Bleh. And then when Sakura and I were walking to the station we stopped in this park and took a nap on the grass, and someone stole her laptop while we slept. So we had to file a police report thing and it took forever. So getting to Brugge took a while and when we got there I was so tired and it was getting dark, but we explored at night anyway.

Then this morning we woke early, ate breakfast (free) and walked to the train station while sightseeing and taking pictures. Brugge is really beautiful. Canals, old, quaint, brick buildings. And the weather was nice. Sunny!

We have been riding trains all day today. It's nine p.m. and we are supposed to get to Hamburg at midnight. Fuuuh. Oh well. We booked a hostel so hopefully it will be okay. I am excited to take a shower. I dunno what else. I've been feeling a bit anxious. That's all.

04 April 2012

Hello from Hamburg! We checked into our hostel last night and went straight to bed, woke at 11:30 a.m. or so, and then I took a shower and shaved and it was amazing. We walked around, took pics, explored the shops. I bought a skirt at H&M and leggings at a different store. Legit.

I have emailed all the people I needed to email and put up our Brussels pics on Facebook, and organized my life in general, I guess. Woohoo. Tomorrow we are going to take a free tour of Hamburg and I am excited.

06 April 2012

Just got to Berlin! It's 4:35 p.m. and Sakura and I are exploring this crazy rundown area with a shit-ton of graffiti. I'm waiting for her because I already saw it all.

We checked into our hostel which is right down the road, and it's really cool. We are sharing a room with a French guy named Blaise and he is attractive. It's sunny and warmish. I have already taken so many pictures, it's ridiculous.

In Hamburg we took the tour and it was hella long but still interesting. Lots of history. Then we explored the area called Schanzenviertel which is liberal, I guess. Lots of cool people and shops. We wished we would have explored there the first day.

We took the train this morning and it was really crowded so we sat in the hallway. It was okay, though. Sakura is taking forever, as usual. A couple people have already asked me for directions and such things, because I'm awesome and don't look like a tourist…

08 April 2012

Holy shit. The night we got here Sakura and I and Blaise went to Watergate and got hella drunk. And basically Blaise and I are now in love. Haha. We danced the whole time and made out. And I slept in his bed. And he has the nicest body ever. Sakura left early because I think she felt like the third wheel, and I felt bad, but we figured it out and it's all okay. We didn't have sex but he touched me, and he is a fucking god in bed. Best I have ever had, literally.

That day though we walked around, just Sakura and I, and we saw the East Side Gallery, which is the largest remaining piece of the Berlin Wall and has a ton of art on it. Real cool.

Today is the ninth actually, but I'm writing in yesterday's entry. Yesterday Sakura got up early and went exploring by herself, so Blaise and I hung out together all day. And I got fucking caught by the ticket inspectors on the train without a ticket and had to pay 40 fucking euros! They made me go to an ATM by the station and take out money! Isn't that horrible?! God, so that made me really anxious and it was bad. But we were still able to have fun and explore.

We went to that building that is completely covered in graffiti and just walked around. Sunny but cold. Oh, I forgot to say that we all went to the Jewish Museum together and it was pretty cool.

Also, last night Blaise and I went to this lounge party thing with these French people he met, and they were so fucking cool. The two guys he met had organized the party and were DJing with turntables, which is what Blaise is into. And everyone is relaxed and the music isn't stupid American pop music, and they smoke and drink and are super nice and are not fake at all. It seriously is the craziest thing to me. I just felt so jealous the whole time. Because that is how I want my life to be: friends, no anxieties, fun. But there are literally no people like that in America. Maybe like Weston, but I dunno.

The French people (and German, there were German people, too) just have the best mindset to me. Like, they were weird! Like, cool weird: different, interesting, unique. And everyone was accepted and accepting, and I loved it.

I seriously think Blaise is the coolest person ever. Because he is fucking hilarious, like we act really dumb together, and he likes hanging out with Sakura and me and how weird we are, and I feel completely myself around him. And then there's the amazing in bed thing…Also he looks so cool: attractive, good clothes, has that piercing on the back of his neck (sexy) and is super open minded. His bandmate is gay and gay doesn't bother him at all, like American people – IDAHO! He told me he's kissed guys, haha. He said he could probably do that even if not drunk.

He smokes and I love the smell of cigarettes and I am attracted to his normal smell, and I am never attracted to guys. He said he likes to be alone and that he doesn't have a girlfriend because he doesn't need girls because he has music and cigarettes and his French accent is hilarious. I just want to live in Berlin for forever and hang out with him and other French and German people.

We leave tomorrow for Munich and I am going to be so fucking sad because I have become attached to him (but not in like an obsessive way, just as a good friend and someone to be affectionate with) and, I dunno. He is seriously the only person so far in my life that I actually am attracted to and was able to hook up with. Like, really. All the guys I've ever hooked up with have liked me way more than I have liked them, to the point where I question if I'm even attracted to them at all. And all the guys who I've found to be extremely attractive I never hooked up with, or after getting to know them I decided I wasn't attracted to them.

I like it because I don't know that Blaise feels the same. He doesn't say, "Come on," or, "I need you," and I love it. I love that he is carefree and doesn't want to be annoyingly obsessed with me. I do need someone that doesn't need me. And he doesn't, and I love it. He's not predictable like all the other guys in the world that only want to fuck me and are boring to hang out with. God.

It's probably good that a real relationship won't be able to grow, because I think I would end up being hurt. Maybe. Because I've never been hurt like that before, or in love with someone. I don't know. It's probs bad, actually. Shit. Fuck. Cocksucker motherfucker!

I like that he rolls his own cigarettes sometimes and also smokes blunts. It's just normal here. Like, in America everyone tries to be so badass or cool or whatever by smoking, and here it's just normal and not arrogant or pretentious at all. It's like people just do what they feel and are sincere and don't say things they don't mean. It's the best thing ever. I want to have friends like that, but no one is ever good enough.

What I want: write book, graduate school somewhere legit?, work in lounge bars or calm places with cool music, live in Berlin…smoke cigarettes and weed, drink, hang out, tattoos, friends that are real. That is all? Dunno.

10 April 2012

In Munich.

Last night was horrible because we could not get in touch with our Couchsurfing host, so we rode the metro all the way to where his house was but didn't know where to go after that and my phone wouldn't work so we went back to the metro and asked this 18-year-old guy for help – Michael – and ended up taking a cab back to the main station with him because the metro closed. And then we just got a hostel instead of trying to Couchsurf.

I am glad because the hostel is cheap and we were able to relax.

12 April 2012

You could be a million, billion different people
but you are *you*.

Soft, creamy, matte finish across green fields
Fields the color of your eyes
A rose tinted sky
Hovering droplets of darkness
Fluffy blue
Speed

How many people will you cherish in this lifetime?
Cigarette burns. Lies.

Chasing the sunset.

16 April 2012

Home in London. This week I'm doing the classroom audits at the university, so right now I'm at campus. I'm sitting outside on a bridge type thing. Alone, cold, crisp, clear. Well, overcast, but the air feels clear and quiet. This morning my career group did our presentation and it went well. I acted very calm and I don't think I got red, haha.

Sakura and I got home on Saturday night and Sunday we got all our film developed, and I got my digital camera fixed, thank god. So many good pictures.

Zurich was alright, the most expensive place I've ever been…We Couchsurfed with this guy named Hernani and he was really nice and accommodating. Good host. Sakura and I climbed to this viewing tower and it just blew my mind; the view was GORGEOUS. Zurich, well, I guess Switzerland in general, is absolutely beautiful. Mountains, lush green, etc., etc.…It wasn't my favorite place, though. The people were kind of snobby it seemed like. I'm glad we were only there for a couple days.

I am feeling kind of down because I miss Blaise and Berlin, and I just feel like he doesn't really miss me. I seriously like him more than I've ever liked anyone. At least, I think I do, just because I could be myself around him and he is totally my type. But I feel like if he did miss me he would Facebook message me, because he doesn't really reply. Just short replies, not really saying anything.

I'm starting to get over him, I guess. I mean, it helps that I've only known him for four days and we haven't really talked since we parted. God.

I feel stupid for writing all this because it's not a big deal, it's just that I hate everyone, and for once in my life I was truly attracted to someone and could learn from him and he was attracted to me back. But my cynicism and doubts are now getting in the way and I feel that he doesn't like me at all. I will forever be alone, and I think I've always thought this, because I push people away, but for once in my life it felt nice to be with another person, to be touched, to be kissed. I usually don't like those things but with him it was okay.

And I wasn't embarrassed by him at all; usually when I'm with a guy I am embarrassed because I am not super attracted to him and I feel like we look strange together, but Blaise was perf. I just wish he would message me back or say something to me, letting me know if he likes me or whatever. God, I don't know.

In Zurich our host showed us a movie called *Berlin Calling* and it was SO GOOD. It was about a DJ in Berlin and the music was so incredible. It just confirmed my desires to be involved with Berlin. I love that whole scene, that vibe, that atmosphere. It felt so good to me, and I want it back.

The sun came out and it's really bright and one side of my face feels hot now. I don't really know how I feel or what I want to be doing. I have two more audits to do and then I will go back to the dorms, I suppose. Homework and such things…

I can only love people that are better than me. God, this hurts. I can't concentrate, I'm trying to work on Health Psych stuff but it just isn't working. I can't stop thinking about Berlin and what Blaise does in his daily life and what he thinks about and if he is with any girls. I'm so annoying. This is painful. He is not having any problems like this, I'm sure of it. Fuck.

Things: wanting to cry when listening to Paul Kalkbrenner's mixes because they are so fucking beautiful, missing Berlin, feeling it in my chest as a physical pain, *Berlin Calling*, how it's a different world, how I want to be a part of that world, how I feel left out, how I need desperately to escape America and the superficial people there, Polaroids, fisheye pics turning out grainy and wonderful, how exciting getting your film developed is, *how I only love people that are alone*, like

Icka in *Berlin Calling* (played by Paul Kalkbrenner), how strange emotion is, how emotion is so tightly linked to music and art,

how Blaise said he was perfectly okay with me, how he said he loves my intelligence, how he said I have the perfect body for him, crunchy Speculoos, how I'll continue writing entries like this in a sketchbook or diary for the rest of my life,

What could the future hold?

17 April 2012

Doing audits again, except in a different building this time. It's alright. Takes a while because there're a million rooms. Everyone here is very artistic, and I keep seeing artwork in all the classrooms I have to go to. That's all, I guess. I have been feeling fat. Feeling that I look fat. Dunno.

Undated

A letter to Blaise that I will never show him, for fear of freaking him out or making him feel other negative emotions:

I would like to not tell you how I feel because I fear you will reject me, or feel disgusted, or fear any attachment. Because that is how I feel with everyone that gets even relatively close to me.

But you, you are different. I found you attractive when I first saw you, not just as a drunken lunatic. And I don't find people attractive. I may think they are physically attractive, but when I talk to them I automatically begin to resent them. Everyone bores me, no one is good enough. Instead, I liked everything you had to say. You are so immensely interesting, so artistic, so uninvolved with things that don't matter. You know what you like and you don't concern yourself with superficial things.

I remember you said you don't need girls because you have your music and I find that so *fucking* attractive. I want you because you don't need me, because you do your own thing, you're independent, you have your own schedule. You value things for their genuineness; you don't simply value appearances. That is so different from things in the US.

You encompass another, better world, the world of *Berlin Calling*, the world I fear I'll never live in.

I LOVE YOU BECAUSE YOU APPEAR TO BE SOLITARY.

alone

I'm already losing you,

I never had you to begin with…

–Ana

20 April 2012

Today I had Research Methods seminar and lecture, and I left lecture early because I just cannot handle it. I'm so sick of how school is set up here. I'm sick of being told to write research reports without them teaching me anything about it. It's so fucking annoying and tedious and boring and pointless. I can't be thorough if they give me absolutely no direction. I feel like I'm getting stupider because I never have assignments or anything to help me retain the information.

And they expect us to write thorough reports with lecture once a week. Not going to happen. I'm just angry and frustrated, I guess. I dunno, I'm tired of doing this shit.

23 April 2012

In Edinburgh. It's really beautiful here! I took the train yesterday and for most of the trip I talked to the British guy next to me. He was going to Newcastle because he goes to school there. Nice guy.

I got here about 3:30 p.m. and checked into my hostel, which is soooo cool. There is art everywhere, lots of people, free wifi and breakfast (I'm at breakfast right now), and cool common room areas. It's just really great. And it's nice to be alone, so relaxing.

It was ridiculously sunny yesterday and beautiful. I saw the castle and walked around the grassy park. So pretty. Thankfully my digital camera works! I also had dinner with Andrea and Jonah and their two friends who are really nice and funny and creative. And have a lot of tattoos. I love it.

I had dreams about Chadwick and soccer last night. Not fun. I was also very sweaty when I woke up. Today I will explore and hopefully go to a vintage store and a cool bookshop. Then probs meet up with Jonah and Andrea later. Well, I guess that's all…

Oh wait, Friday night Sakura and I attempted to go to the Big Chill Bar in Shoreditch and ended up riding buses all night, completely lost. Haha. And we went to this random place we found for like 20 minutes. And I made out with this white South African guy and some other guy I thought was gay at first, and then left. Ha, it was so dumb. Okay, that's all.

24 April 2012

Leaving today at two. It's raining. Thank god it decided to rain today instead of while I was exploring. It rained a bit yesterday but I got a Costa coffee and it was perf. I had a dream last night that Trevor from the guys' soccer team in Seattle sent me a package in London and it was just blueberries. Haha, it was so weird.

I am once again drinking coffee at free breakfast. Yesterday I went to a vintage store and a used bookstore, and I bought three books for £8, it was awesome. I also hung out with Jonah and Andrea and then had dinner at this pub, and the service kind of sucked. Oh well. I also visited this park for a bit. They have those cherry blossom trees everywhere here and they're so beautiful! Well, I guess that is all.

Oh, I forgot, I finished reading *Dorian Gray* last night. That book was weird as fuck, haha. I'm going to begin one of the books I bought yesterday. Woo.

27 April 2012

Home in London. I got back on Tuesday, had class on Wednesday, Thursday I tried to see what was wrong with Digit-Chan, my Holga camera (nothing, they say, but I know there is because the left side of my pics are always blurry), and today is Friday. I went to my Research Methods seminar and skipped Health Psych and took a six-hour nap instead. Great. Now it's a quarter to one a.m. and I'm wide awake.

Edinburgh was great, I'm glad I got to go. Before I left we went to the Camera Obscura & World of Illusions place. It wasn't that cool, actually. Way overpriced. Oh well. Andrea didn't make me pay for the train to and from Edinburgh, and she paid for like all my dinners with them. It was absolutely ridiculous; she spoils me so much. It's great. She is so nice and funny. I am happy to know them.

Anyway, tomorrow I am going to try to get a shit-ton of homework done. I have to print a ton of stuff and pick up my first practical report for Research Methods. I really think I got a horrible grade. Oh well, that class is fucking stupid. Okay, well, I guess that is all.

29 April 2012

I'm at the café in Blitz with Sakura, doing homework. I'm sick and congested and gross. Yesterday I packed a ton of shit to send home and recycled lots of stuff, and washed my clothes. It felt good. I've been feeling sort of anxious lately. About money and where I'm going to travel after school is over and how I will travel. I feel like my best option would be to get a Eurail pass, but I'm not sure…

30 April 2012

Today was really good. It was sunny and nice and I just felt happy and excited about life. Everything seemed to work out. I got a Couchsurfing invite for Athens (woo!), our seminar prof bought us coffee because there was a fire drill and we had to leave the building, I got my first Research Methods practical back and I got an A on it, and Mom agreed to my epic summer travel plans, which require a Eurail Global pass that costs $775. Whoa. And my academic advisor emailed me back and I'm pretty sure I know what classes I want to take in the fall, back in Boise. And everyone I see seems to be in a good mood; they either smile, or if it's a guy they check me out. Haha.

I am going to see Blaise again because I'm going to Berlin again (hopefully it all works out) and I'm so happy because I am so motherfucking in love with him. Also, it's spring and everything is green and lush and gorgeous and I adore it. It feels so right, like this is the way life is supposed to be. It feels like when I was little and I would wake in my bed before elementary school and hear the sounds of cars and birds and the world outside my window. It would be so calm and getting lighter outside but the sun hadn't risen yet. I love hearing the birds sing. I love how vibrant the leaves of the trees are. I feel the world changing and pulsing and growing, and it feels so safe.

I feel like time has flown by so quickly, I remember all the things I've done in London, in Europe. The days stay lighter much longer now and it makes everything better. The days last longer, there are more things to do, more time to spend outside. I guess that's all for now. I think I'm going to take a short nap.

04 May 2012

I love how when you're traveling you wear things you'd never usually wear.

05 May 2012

It's seven p.m. and I'm in a KFC in Bristol. I found a Couchsurfing host for tonight so I don't have to be homeless. He is like 30 and from India. And really quiet. He works all night tonight, so he won't be there until four a.m. But he is going to let me into the apartment at nine p.m. when he gets a break. So until then I'm just hanging out.

I walked around Bristol today after I got here, and it's nice here. Calm, artistic, by the water. I hung out in a Café Nero and in a Starbucks, and didn't buy anything. I've been trying to write my Health Psych case study, but it's really stupid. I'll probs just bullshit the rest of it because it's not even counting for anything at BSU. At least I don't think it is.

I'm glad I don't have to be homeless tonight. I'm tired. Last night I got drunk and Sakura and I went to the karaoke thing downstairs but there were barely any people there. We didn't go out, so I watched a movie and ate a ton of caramel digestives and then was mad at myself for doing that.

I've been thinking a lot lately. I feel really anxious and down. And lonely. I need someone to talk to that isn't Sakura. I miss Blaise and I feel like he doesn't miss me at all. He was so real, and when I leave Berlin I'm going to be so fucking depressed. All over again. I'm lonely but no one is good enough. I want to hang out with interesting people, but there aren't any. I hate everyone; they bore me. What else…

I don't know what I want. In life. I'm going to travel all summer and I think I'm happy about it. Not excited to go back to Boise, but I dunno what I would want to do instead. I think life is about being with other people, but what if other people don't interest you? I dunno…I think I'm going to read my book.

06 May 2012

Last night I slept on this teeny couch at the Couchsurfing guy's house, and it was totally fine. He was gone all night so I got to be alone and it was so relaxing and quiet.

Today I woke around 11 and got up and went to my hostel, which is like part of a bowling alley. I went to Primark and spent £13 on a bra, shorts, sandals, travel bottles for shampoo and stuff, and these glue-on nails with the Union Jack on them. Really good deal! I needed these things, you see.

I also walked all over Bristol. I walked to and across the suspension bridge, which I guess is famous or something. Beautiful out, not too cold. Tomorrow I'm going to go on a Banksy scavenger hunt. By myself. I figured out where they are according to my map.

I was alone in the hostel room for the whole day (I mean, I was alone whenever I was there, I wasn't there the whole day), except for like three minutes these French guys came in and I talked to one of them for a bit. He's living in Birmingham and working as a translator. Neat.

I didn't realize it's like 10 p.m. right now. Weird. I've been working on my case study report and I made a lot of progress. It's colossal bullshit. I guess that's all.

Undated

I want to learn to fight, to hunt, to survive in the wilderness. To survive in a dead city, to survive when everyone else is gone, to survive alone, to survive in exile.

I need this.

No matter what happens, you will always have somewhere to sleep, you will always have something to eat. What's the problem? You feel like you're going to die. But you won't. What's the problem?

09 May 2012

I'm home from Bristol. I ended up hanging out with the French guys all day while searching for Banksy artwork. We didn't find them all but it's okay. We got distracted by a beer festival thing on the water and got drunk instead. Ha. I ended up sleeping with one of them, Damien, the one living in Birmingham. He was cute. He slept in my bed. And we didn't really have sex. He gave me a massive hickey, though. I really liked hanging out with them. So nice and funny.

The train ride home was relaxing. Yesterday I was on my laptop *all* day uploading pictures and stuff. I think I'm done with my case study…It's really bad. I now have one paper left to write. Aesthetics. Ugh.

Tonight is the London Eye and dinner for study abroad! Sakura isn't going because she couldn't get a ticket. We are also going to the Natural History Museum. I'll probably go straight to the London Eye from there. I dunno. Well, I suppose that's all…

12 May 2012

Yesterday I did nothing. I slept, was on my laptop all day, couldn't sleep at night. Felt fat and horrible. I made a bit of progress on my Aesthetics essay, but I dunno.

Today is beautiful. I'm going to run to Camden.

Oh, I turned in my case study and career shit, so glad that's over with.

I am so sick of living here, with Moe. She's starting to drive me insane, her stupid little irks and fucking quirks. I don't know where to go to study or be alone. I have no friends except Sakura and she is making me insane. Maybe it's Japanese people in general, who knows. Ugh. Nothing else.

14 May 2012

I love when the coffee I make in the morning is perfect.

Yesterday I went to bed around five a.m., and it was getting light, really light, and it felt strange.

I walked to Camden and Primrose Hill as well because it was sunny and beautiful. This clearly drunk black guy jumped up from his sitting position with his friend when I walked by them on the canal and asked me where I was from and if I was single. I said no even though I'm totally forever alone. He was gross. Everyone stared at me, and yesterday I looked really good, ha. I love the attention. Seriously. I wonder if that's bad…

I feel like I'm just waiting impatiently for the days to go by so I can travel. And meet other people. And not be chronically bored. ENNUI.

I made much progress on my Aesthetics essay last night at like three a.m.

I feel like I haven't been saying any of the things that need to be said. Just in here, for my own mental wellbeing. I've been realizing more and more, just through small interactions with others, that I'm a loner. Like REALLY. I hate working with others. Or traveling. Especially traveling. Because they always take the lead and go the slow way. Or the long way. Or wrong way. Like when I took the tube with Brian and Ashley to the study abroad dinner. Brian just took the lead and I was like…yeah, this is definitely the long way. Great, you are STUPID and I am fucking street smart like a ninja secret agent, and I can't stand other people slowing me down.

I like to wear all black with my hood up and walk quickly, silently, smoothly, passing through crowds as a shadow, as a vague, dark presence, sensing everything, absorbing, perceiving, observing, quietly passing into and out of existence. Alone. Alone, yet great. Alone, yet important. Misunderstood. Tragic. People bore me anyway. Sometimes I need them, but after a while I'm like, "Okay, next." Boring.

I do what I want, I get what I need, I use the English language beautifully, I embrace the vibrations other people give off. So fucking socially perceptive, that's me.* I know what you're thinking. It's the eyes, the expression.

[*Ana: Yeah, you've got Venus in Aquarius in the first house. –J.]

15 May 2012

disappointment, going back to America as degeneration, loneliness?, maybe not, coffee and cigarettes, wine and cheese and chocolate, annoyed with Moe's lack of social perception, disbelief at how people are horrible at perceiving others' feelings and emotions, long nails, long hair, gray clouds, slowly shifting skies, how incredible my life is, how American people don't understand anything, sick of living in this little box, there's nowhere to go, I'm trapped and I can't do anything about it

Can you really trust your mind?

Can you trust *anyone*?

Undated

To Blaise:

You don't need me. I need you for just this moment. I fear commitment and I'd never ask someone to be mine, for them as well as me. How could I ask that of someone? It seems selfish, intruding. Besides, there's never been anyone I've wanted. To want, for me, is to admire, to look up to, to want to be like. That's you, really, it is. I understand you are a loner, but it's okay because I am, too. How perfect to meet someone that gives me space, isn't clingy, isn't dependent. You know how refreshing that is? Do you know how incredibly rare that is for me?

I can't be around people for too long, they make me fucking crazy. Which is why I like you, because you wouldn't want to be constantly with me. You probably don't even like me…which I kind of like. People bore me with their superficial talk, strong emotions about useless, futile things. Unimportant things.

I need a mind that can match mine. I need anger, fear, despair. But not always. But I still need it. Maybe a little insanity on the side. Who knows? You gotta spice it up sometimes. I don't know you nearly enough to judge whether you fit the requirements, but there's a vibe you give off that intrigues me. It's…loneliness. But contentment.

You told me once that you don't need girls. You have your music, you don't have time for a girlfriend. Do you know how happy that makes me? Do you know how much I love that you don't need me? I adore your mindset. Do you know how amazing a specimen you are? Honestly, I think I'm completely in love with you, but I don't ask you to love me back. I don't ask you for anything, maybe to just be my friend.

I love being around you because you respect me. As a person. Not as a girl you only want to fuck. You know, a lot of guys like me, but they're all so fucking stupid. I'll fuck them, sometimes, only because I'm so fucking bored, chronically bored, ennui. But I don't care about them because they don't understand. Anything. I like the attention, but I drop them quickly because they irritate me. They just want to have sex, and that bores me. It's not fun for me.

I need a mind. I need a mental connection, respect, understanding. What I don't want is commitment, loyalty. That annoys me. I want truth. I love that you probably sleep with other girls, but will still let me live in your flat for a week and be kind to me.

In America there are so many people that don't seem genuine. It's why I love Europe and don't want to go back home. People here do what they want and aren't self-conscious or sarcastic about it. Or embarrassed or hypocritical. In America they are, and I hate it. I like your genuineness. I like your music and your style and your intelligence and open-mindedness. And independence. I like that I don't know you enough to say any of these things to you, but I still am.

Hopefully you won't think I'm a fucking psychopath…I probably am. I'm not sure yet if I will give you this letter or just throw it away…

I want to say thank you in advance for saying I can stay in your flat (and if you change your mind that is okay). The last thing I want is to be annoying or distracting to you, so I don't expect you to hang out with me at all moments. Anyway, I do mostly everything on my own so it's not a big deal. I'm not expecting anything, really, so don't feel you have to do anything differently when I'm there. I'm just in love with Berlin's vibes, they'll keep me alive, I need them.

I'm probably perceiving you inaccurately. I'm probably creating a personality for you based on my inward desires and judgments not based on fact. I wonder if you could tell me if I'm right or not? I wonder if you could tell me what's really in your mind?

–Ana

20 May 2012

Haven't written in a while. I finished my Aesthetics essay and am going to turn it in tomorrow. I also had my Research Methods exam and it was alright. I don't think I got an A, but I don't think I failed…Maybe a C. Or just passing. I don't even care.

I have been watching *The Walking Dead*, and I am just in love with Norman Reedus. I want to be in love with someone that I meet in strange circumstances (like the zombie apocalypse) and not somewhere boring like at university or when guys approach me because they just want to fuck me. Boring.

Blaise told me he got a job in Tunisia for all of June, and so I won't be able to stay with him in Berlin. Sad face. I was so in love with him. I think. But he never really talked to me that much after we parted, like on Facebook. And I think I am over him now. It took like a month or so, but I think I am over him. Imagine if we had actually been dating for a long time, how long it would have taken me to get over him if we broke up. I only knew him for four days! I think it was the whole lifestyle, though –

Berlin, club music, cigarettes and coffee, French, creativity, nice people. I had to get over all of that.

But I'm going back to Berlin anyway and I am excited, and hopefully I'll meet new, interesting people. I'm not sure yet if I'll Couchsurf, but I kind of don't want to in Berlin. I dunno…

21 May 2012

Today I am turning in my paper! And then I am going on a mission for Andrea in Soho and maybe Camden. She needs buttons and charms for a project for Maya. It will be cute I think.

Last night I got rid of a ton of shit from my suitcases, and this guy knocked on our door and told me that he and his friend saw me packing through my window and wanted to know if I was moving somewhere in London. And then he said that they wanted to be friends or something with me. And I was just so confused and surprised, haha. Like…um, creepy? But at the same time he was trying to not make it apparent that they find me attractive, and I liked that. It takes balls to knock on a girl's door like that and have a real conversation. It was just super funny and strange.

I dunno what else. I'm drinking coffee and being very happy about it. Tomorrow I am going to take all my stuff to Jonah and Andrea's and send it home. I think it will be my last visit to their house. Okay, that's all, bye!

Boondock Saints: I dunno what it is about him, but I am so much more in love with Norman Reedus than Sean Patrick Flannery, even though SPF is skinnier, in the stomach at least…what is it? What is it?

24 May 2012

What I want: an everlasting spring, to sit at a tiny table outside of cafés, drinking coffee, smoking cigarettes, reading or writing. Skinny arms, long hair, long nails, zombie apocalypse, Norman Reedus or someone like him

The last couple days I have been at Jonah and Andrea's. It was fun. Hot and humid out! I read a lot of my book while there, and today we watched *The Addams Family*, which I had actually never seen. It was pretty funny. They dropped me off at the train station…

When I got back to London I just organized my stuff a bit and took a shower because I was horribly sweaty and revolting. I also walked to the park-ish thing right by the dorms and smoked three cigarettes while contemplating life. This weird guy parked his car in the middle of the street and asked to borrow my lighter, and then tried to like invite himself to sit and talk with me and I said no. Ha. I swear, guys are so eager to ditch all of their friends to talk to me; he was just going to leave his friend that was with him in his car. It's so annoying, what happened to the bro code?

Anyway, I started that "what I want" list and didn't finish because my pen ran out, so now I will resume: a Space Invader tattoo on my left leg, above the knee, my own studio apartment where I can live alone and not have very many things. I dunno what else…my train of thought got fucked up by my pen and I can't get it back now. I'll write later.

25 May 2012

Cooling down in Café Nero, it's hot hot hot! I had a massive headache and needed coffee. Today I bought three books at a cheap bookshop and over-the-knee, black, opaque socks because I am getting blisters on my feet from my Primark sandals and I needed socks! Also, I have been wanting over-the-knee socks like that. Only bad thing was they cost £12. American Apparel. Holy shit. I kind of want a sweet fanny pack.

Blood, Björk, and Brainwashing: A catalogue of ideas, thoughts, curiosities, and desires of one insignificant human, written in the first person.

I love scissors, zip-lock bags, film canisters, organizing, maps, tampons, cheap bookstores, fake tattoos, watching movies online, cutting up tights to make socks and black chokers, fake sugar, being fucking prepared for everything ever, this red pen, finding things, using exact change when paying for something, spring, warm breezes, finishing a book, making lists, having limited options for outfits and jewelry, frugality, the deep muskiness of the sun in the late afternoon,

nails with the tips painted black, anticipation and excitement about traveling, using things up and throwing them away, meeting people to hang out with for only one city, not staying in one place for longer than a week, not having a real home, exploring every day, walking everywhere, smoking cigarettes instead of eating, coffee coffee coffee, pencils, learning, wearing things out, being self-sufficient, watching people watch me…

27 May 2012

In Dublin! It's so sunny and beautiful. Warm! The hostel is kind of shitty but I am alone in the room. Yesterday there were three other girls but they all left today. One was studying English here, from Brazil, and the other was Japanese. I didn't talk to the third one…

I took the ferry here and then walked from the ferry all the way to the hostel, worst idea ever. Took forever and my stuff was so heavy because I had a lot of food. But it's okay now. Oh, and the inside of my legs chafe and it's not pleasant. It's horrible, actually, but I just have to deal with it. I think I got a bit sunburnt today. Which is really funny to say!

Tomorrow I am going to do a free tour, and on Tuesday I think I'm going to do the shrooms that Kan and I bought in Amsterdam…Hopefully, because I need to get rid of them before I fly to Berlin. Do *not* want to get caught by airport security. Well, I dunno what else, went to Primark and bought a purse and new black shoes – oh, it's called Penneys here, not Primark. Okay, I think I'm going to take a shower now.

30 May 2012

I am so incredibly frustrated right now. I am trying to get to Belfast by train. If you buy a ticket online it costs £9. If you buy it at the station it costs £28. So I am trying to buy it online. I spent two euros at the station for 20 minutes of internet, which was really slow and used up half my time trying to load. So I decided to find internet somewhere else. Which means I needed to buy a UK adapter because I brought my mainland Europe one. So I did, and now I am in a café that has free wifi, but my laptop will not connect to it for some unknown reason. So I made a free account with a really shitty wifi, and I think I only have 30 minutes and it's taking forever, and it's SO FUCKING FRUSTRATING WHY DOES NOTHING EVER WORK WITH THE FUCKING INTERNET!?!?!?

Also, the website that is like the main website for buying tickets won't let me buy a ticket from Dublin to Belfast, which I need. It will only let me go from Belfast to Dublin. And so I searched a different website, and it was working for a bit, and I put my debit card info in, and now it won't work anymore, so I'm just waiting for it to decide to work. Ugh.

Anyway, I did the free tour; it was very interesting and the tour guide was funny. A true Irish guy, my age with dark red hair. It was sunny and awesome so they took our picture for the website. I didn't do shrooms yesterday because it wasn't sunny. Instead I went to the Gardens of Remembrance, walked along the canal, and finished my book! Drank a Guinness and a cider, and bought sunscreen and cigarettes, seven euros, yikes.

Okay, safe in Belfast! Finally. I was finally able to buy my train tickets, and the train ride was good. I walked to the hostel, got a bit lost but not bad. This hostel is better than Dublin's; there's a kitchen and a common room, so I'll be able to eat oatmeal and make my own coffee and such. I got to the hostel around 5:30 or six p.m., took a shower, and went out walking around the city. My feet started to hurt and I started feeling faint so I bought a croissant and a bag of crisps and some apple juice. They use pounds instead of euros here. I didn't know that until the hostel guy was like, "Um, these are euros, do you have pounds?" Ha.

Oh, I am in a room with one girl; she is from Dublin and looking for a job here. She's nice. All the other people I've seen in the hostel seem really snobby. I haven't talked to anyone. There are a lot of non-native English speakers. Some German girls are playing cards at the other table, and there were French girls in here earlier. I'm just so jealous of their multilingual abilities. There is a TV in the kitchen.

I've noticed Irish girls are homely as fuck! And the guys aren't that much better. It's funny. The girls wear *so much* foundation, to cover up their ugliness. It doesn't work. Ha, I'm mean. But it's true. And it's not like I'm gorgeous or anything so it doesn't matter. I dunno how that justifies it, but it does.

I made a new FB album of my Ireland pics. So far there are more than 200 pics, wowza! I'm not sure if I really like Belfast. Irish people seem very friendly, but Belfast is kind of boring. Pretty by the water, though. Also, mostly everything was closed because I was wandering around after five, so maybe tomorrow it will be livelier. Dublin was cool but it felt inauthentic because it was super touristy. I think I spent the perfect amount of time there, and I think only 2.5 days in Belfast is perf as well. We will see.

Undated

This is a demonstration of my lust for immortality. Narcissism may be a contributor as well.

Everything needs to mean something, everything should have a purpose, or else it feels useless to me.

Things I can't figure out:

1. Why guys want to hang out with girls – do they ever actually find girls to be interesting? Or do they only want to fuck them? Because most of

the girls I know are fucking annoying and stupid and not interesting at all. Okay, not most, but a lot.*

[*Ana: Um, it's not just girls; it's guys, too, that are annoying and stupid. It's people. It's literally just that most people are annoying and stupid. Haha. But seriously. You immediately assuming that it's girls that are annoying and stupid is internalized misogyny. Have any of the guys you've been interacting with lately seem actually interesting, other than Blaise? Your question is relevant, though. From your perspective it seems that guys only want to have sex and aren't interested in anything else. I think it's just the age you're at. Everyone wants to get laid, both guys and girls. –J.]

2. How I should feel about homeless people. How I should feel about the way people have homes and jobs and food and money. The way people survive and are interested in particular things. I feel that I must know how to survive in a completely self-reliant way, or else I am weak, or stupid, or would die when the zombie apocalypse comes. I don't want to just buy everything I want or need because that concept, the concept of money, is just weird and I don't trust it. It seems almost too easy, or deceitful in a way.

What happens when the system crashes? What do you do when money no longer gets you what you want?* How can you be interested in other things when you don't even know how to survive on your own? Are homeless people bad or wrong or stupid? IDK.

[*Ana: I think what you really want is to not need money at all. It'd be nice if everyone grew their own food and relied on locally produced necessary items – like how indigenous people lived before European settlers ruined everything. One's life would feel purposeful if one wasn't coerced into being a wage slave to some random exploitative corporation (that is probably actively destroying the environment and not contributing to the good of society, but only to the richest one percent), and instead could focus on helping to produce things that are actually necessary to life, like food, shelter, and education for everyone.

Homeless people aren't bad, wrong, or stupid. Maybe some of them are, but certainly not all of them. And we could say the same of people that live in homes. Homeless people have slipped through the cracks of society, because modern society doesn't serve everyone. Maybe they are sick and can't get the right medication because it's too expensive and because of that they are unable to function in the way society views as appropriate. Maybe they come from poverty and abusive family situations and can't figure out how to escape them. Maybe they are drug addicts because they could only get access to the wrong kind of drug to make them feel better, and again can't get help because it was never available to them. Maybe they like being homeless because it's freeing to sleep under the stars without a tent and walk in the moonlight and they don't want to work a job they hate. Maybe it's all of these things. The possibilities are limitless. To say that all homeless people are bad or wrong or stupid is like saying that all men like hunting or that all women paint their nails. It's a stereotype that betrays a person's ignorance. –J.]

3. Relationships, loyalty, being able to truly trust someone else. How can you really know another person? Or trust them to keep your secrets or stay loyal? I feel you can't. I feel it's impossible and therefore futile to attempt to create these relationships, at least with a person of the opposite sex. I don't feel that someone that wants to fuck you can ever be trusted. I want a *mind*, and men want a *body*. How can this ever work out? It makes no sense, it feels irrational.

04 June 2012

It's June! Yesterday I checked out of the dorms; it was surprisingly easy. I'm done with school and am going to travel for the summer now.

From Belfast I went to Dublin and stayed at a hostel by the Connolly train station, and the next morning woke early and walked to the ferry. Took forevs, but at the end a cab driver drove me the rest of the way for free. He said I was his good deed for the day.

Last night I stayed at Arsenal Tavern in London, and right now I'm waiting for 3:55 to come so I can ride the EasyBus to the airport. In a café, the only customer currently. I have been reading a book called *Rivers of London*, and it is SO GOOD. Hilarious. I dunno what else, I don't think anything crazy has happened…Okay byez.

Undated

London, it's been a brilliant adventure, but I must say goodbye. I have found a new lover. Hello Berlin <3 Third time's a charm?

06 June 2012

Yesterday was my first day in Berlin and I went to Prenzlauer Berg and explored. Today so far I have been to Garage – the secondhand store – and a cemetery. Just walking around. Today I have talked to more people in my hostel than yesterday and I am happier. I think I felt lonely and not a part of Berlin. I'm finding it extremely hard to concentrate on writing this, so I'm going to go, I think. FUCK.

Undated

We met in a hostel in Berlin. It could have been a beautiful love story, but after four days I left for Munich and rode the train floundering in my melancholy while listening to the French rap group he showed me.

Why do I forget the things people tell me?

I forget the things people tell me.

Imagine yourself in the eyes of strangers, forget what people tell you, rearrange the words until it sounds right, do drugs,

12 June 2012

Second day in Athens. Right now I am sitting outside Club Crepe in Exharia, this really cool part of Athens. Alternative. I am full, just had the best meal of my life. Cheese, egg, bacon, sausage, mushroom crepe. To die for.* I'm totally sunburnt, but I bought sunscreen today and I am now wearing it.

[*Ana: Literally! Animals died so you could eat that meal. Was it worth their suffering? Can you imagine yourself in their place? Could you do the slitting of throats yourself? If not, do you deserve to eat their flesh? This goes back to the discussion of money; you use money to pay for someone else to kill animals, so you can eat their flesh and secretions, when you could never kill them yourself. You won't do the dirty work, but will happily partake in exploitation. Do you view yourself as compassionate? As ethical? As a good person? Then do the right thing and either do the dirty work yourself like indigenous people have always done (respectfully, sustainably, and without wasting any part of the animal), or quit participating in violence. –J.]

I met this German girl named Lina on my way to the Acropolis, and we hung out all day, and she is really nice. We might hang out tomorrow. The Acropolis was pretty sweet, too.

I'm Couchsurfing and my host is this 38-year-old Greek guy and he's hilarious. I got lost on the way to his house yesterday after exploring Plaka, and his brother came and picked me up on his motorcycle, it was awesome. Everyone here rides motorcycles, it's sweet. I have my own room, which I have to climb a narrow spiral staircase to get to, it's so cool.

I don't remember when I wrote last. We went to Kater Holzig and Berghain in Berlin. Partied till eight a.m. I did MDMA and speed but I dunno if I felt it. Kareena, the Indian girl, and I hung out with Simon, one of the guys that worked at the hostel. He was British and pretty cool.

The flight to Athens sucked because I had to throw my sunscreen away because I forgot it was a liquid. And I couldn't sleep the night before.

There are stray dogs EVERYWHERE here. Like big, furry, awesome dogs. Also, all the Greek people are super friendly and start conversations with me and hit on me. It's funny and sometimes annoying. Like yesterday I was talking to this 31-year-old guy who was actually attractive, but he had a daughter…He said "big souls meet again" which I liked. And then this old guy wouldn't leave me alone until I told him that we had to part ways, but it took a while to convince him.

When I first started walking around here I almost got run over like 80 times, because it's madness! Sometimes there are no sidewalks, and people park all over the place, like not in designated areas or areas where one would intuitively know you could park there. So disorderly. I've gotten used to it now but at first I was like what is going on!? Okay, I think I am going to explore more now!

16 June 2012

Holy shit I haven't written in forever! I'm in Sofia, Bulgaria. It's around eight p.m. and I'm sitting on a bench in this tiny park on the street behind my hostel. It's a bit chilly now. Kids everywhere. All I can think about is how Mom looked when she was little, and how I played with Camila and Maddie and the farm kids in Grandma's backyard in dirty clothes. And how when you're little you get so dirty and scraped up and tangled. You climb trees and it's later in the evening but the sun's still up and the adults are talking and drinking. As a child you have this safe little world and secret friendships and crushes on your cousins, and it's so wonderful and full. I really feel that here, it's lovely. Bulgarian people are so attractive to me. Both genders!

17 June 2012

Okay. The time is now, I will tell everything. Starting with in Berlin where I left off. I met a girl named Kareena who is from India but studied in London like me, and we realized that we lived across the street from each other in London! And we totally bonded and hung out a lot. One night we went to the club Kater Holzig and met Simon, the British guy that works in our hostel and is really buff and has tattoos, and he shared his MDMA with us, and later he gave me some speed* in the bathroom at Berghain.

[*Ana: Honestly I don't know what it was, but I think it was probably just cocaine. I think when people say "speed" they are meaning meth, and I highly doubt that was meth that he gave you. Either way, there weren't any truly noticeable or interesting effects, so my guess, having much more life experience at this point (04.25.2023, 18:00, Boise, ID) is that it was just cocaine. –J.]

And yeah, we went to Berghain! It was fucking awesome. I love that world. People stay there for a couple days at a time, dancing and heads full of crack. It's madness. Oh, and before that Kareena and I went on an alternative pub crawl and went to all these ridiculous places, like a ping-pong bar and a, like, death metal bar or something. At the end we went to Kaffee Burger, which was right next door to our hostel and they played awesome polka music and we couldn't figure out how to dance. It was hilarious.

We made friends with some Swedish guys, Pontus and Michael, and I kissed Michael once but Pontus and I kissed way more. He wore all black and is in love with Nine Inch Nails, which I like about him a lot. He ended up sleeping in my bed at the hostel, it was great. We fooled around in the bathroom and I asked him to come on my face because I've never experienced that and it was funny. Because he did. And then he had to leave in the morning, leave Berlin.

I flew to Athens and it sucked because I had a ton of shit and didn't check a bag, and I forgot about my sunscreen so I had to throw away the whole bottle. And had to buy plastic baggies to put my liquids in. I didn't get any sleep the night before and had to wake up at five or 4:30 or something horrible.

Athens was hot as fuck, and desolate, and bleached white. And touristy. I actually didn't particularly like it. I liked the area called Exharia because it wasn't touristy and there were tons of unique, interesting people with tats and such, lots of graffiti, and I ate the best crepe of my entire life there at a place called Club Crepe Xharia.

My Couchsurfing host was awesome. Nice, funny. We didn't hang out much because he had to work and I always came back late. The house was so cool; I had to climb up a spiral staircase to get to my room, which had a huge and comfortable bed and my own bathroom. It was cool.

I wish I had stayed in central Athens though, because it sucked having to ride a bus into the city and having to be prepared for a whole day out. But at the same time it was cool to see real neighborhoods and stuff.

All the men were ugly, creepy, fat, hairy, and stared at me. Annoying. I went to the beach once and men like that were in speedos, it was horrible. The beach was rockier than I would have liked, but it was still the ocean. I didn't get all the way in the water because I was wearing a pale pink dress that would have been see-through. That reminds me, I forgot to say that in Berlin Kareena and I went to this sweet flea market in Mauer Park, where I got that dress for five euros. I also got skeleton keys and an ankh for jewelry, a ring for three euros, and food.

In Athens I met a girl named Lina who was really nice, from Germany, and we talked about psychology and lots of interesting things. We are complete opposites; she loves America and I love Europe. We saw the Acropolis together and also the National Gardens the next day. I climbed Filopappos hill, hot but lots of shade. I got super sick of Athens and wanted to leave for Thessaloniki but I could only take the midnight train, so I waited all day in Starbucks watching movies on my laptop, and then took the train, which was like seven hours long.

I met this Greek guy on the train who has the same birthday as me! His name is Orestis and he asked if I wanted to have sex with him in the bathroom. I didn't, but he was absolutely hilarious. He helped me find the bus to Sofia (I just wanted out of Greece and decided to skip

Thessaloniki) and he bought me a frappe. And then I took a bus for like six hours, way better than the train surprisingly, and arrived in Sofia, where although I tried to avoid the taxi driver scammers, I still managed to get scammed. But I didn't give him the 47 lev he demanded, which was way over a normal price for a taxi ride to the hostel, even though he grabbed my bag and tried to not let me out of the car. I gave him a 10 even though that was even too much. I should have not given him anything.

Now I live in a loft of 16 beds and I checked in first so I got the one by the fan, woohoo.

Yesterday I walked around a bit and met these stupid Arab British Canadian guys who I went to the park with for like 10 minutes, and then I left because they were rude and called me a stupid American because I didn't know where Toronto is, and because I said "I don't know" when they asked me the trick question "What's the capital of Africa?" So I went to the other park behind my hostel.

Then when I got back I went to the reception area common room to get tea, but was intercepted by these Canadians that were on the same train and bus as me, and they gave me some Jack Daniels, haha. We hung out with other random hostel people, went on a "pub crawl" sort of, and basically I got drunk for free and never bought anything. It was weird. I met a lot of people but didn't really bond with anyone.

Me and three other guys left the pub crawl and went to this candle bar, but it was, like, completely silent and felt romantic. It was weird. Then we came back to the hostel and I went to bed. I woke today at 11:53 when I meant to wake at 9:30. Whoops.

Anyway, so far I really like Sofia. Guys don't stare at me, it feels calm, it's cheap as hell. I dunno. I just like it. Today I took a massive shit, so I know the day will be awesome. Okay, that's all for now I guess! Write more later.

18 June 2012

Today I walked to the train station to make a reservation for a train to Bucaresti, my next destination! I also went to a market called the Lady's Market. It was mostly food, which I don't really care about, but I took a lot of good pics. Then I came back to the hostel, and bought a watch at the little shop next door.

Yesterday I went on the free tour and it was pretty interesting. I also went to the Sofia mall, and there is a huge grocery store at the bottom, it was amazing! It was basically like an American store, totally blew my mind. It was better than grocery stores in London! It was crazy. I think I'm going to go back today and get headphones, because I remember seeing an electronic store. Okay, I think that's all so far.

Undated

I will never understand travelers that feel they need to wear legit hiking boots to travel, or that carry all their shit with them while walking around. That's what the hostel is for: a place to leave all your stuff while exploring. Also, hiking boots, seriously? You aren't climbing mountains every day…makes no sense to me.

I think living in so many hostels is helping me figure out where I would want to live permanently (semi-permanently) – what kinds of houses/flats, location, climate, etc. I want to live in a small flat with big windows and a balcony, not facing east/west, close to public transportation and in a colder place.

What's important is the vibrations emanating from where you live and how you live.

21 June 2012

Bucharest: more humid, cloudier, better architecture, bigger than Sofia. No burning cars, no gypsy children. I rather like it here. I took the train from 9 a.m. to 8:30 p.m. yesterday, it sucked! But the windows opened so I just stood with my arms and head in the wind, it was nice. I also met this 40-something year old guy named Chris from Philadelphia on the train, and we talked a lot and it was good to talk to an American. He didn't seem that old. He was kind of a badass and reminded me of Sawyer.

The hostel was super easy to find and the people are nice. But the room last night was SO FUCKING HOT. It was humid and I woke up the Korean girl by the window so she could open it. Other than that nothing bad happened.

This morning this Nigerian guy studying international business talked to me, and he hit on me, and I am so not attracted to him, and he kind of ruined my morning ritual of coffee and figuring out my life and reading. I just had to get away from him so my ritual wasn't completed. Annoying.

Today I walked around a couple parks. One had this kickass play castle thing for kids that was insanely huge, it was amazing. Then I walked around the city a bit. I want to do a tour eventually. Bucharest has the sweetest buildings! They are all castle-like or weirdly shaped or old and falling apart or massive. So cool.

In Sofia I did end up going to the mall again, and I got amazing headphones for 16 lev, which is like 11 dollars, I think. Awesome. I just kind of hung out and walked around and did nothing in particular the last day I was there. I went to parks and such, dunno.

The people in Bucharest seem more advanced than Sofia. Teen girls are more fashionable I think, and also way more people speak English. I've already taken a ton of awesome pics.

Last night I Skyped Kareena and she told me about her last days in Berlin; they sounded fun. I LOVE BERLIN! But this guy she met that she hit it off with stood her up the next day and never called her back or anything, just left her hanging. I totally thought of Blaise, and I felt way better knowing that someone else experienced basically the same thing and felt mindfucked and confused. I mean, he didn't stand me up technically, but I do kind of feel like he made up the whole job in Tunisia thing so he wouldn't have to host me. I dunno, I just feel like we hit it off and then he never really talked to me again after that. Whatever.

Right now I'm in KFC because I couldn't find a coffee place and I was hungry. I dunno what else I'm going to do. Kind of tired…but I don't really want to go back to the hostel because that Nigerian guy might be there and it's kind of hot there. I'll probs read my book here for a while.

24 June 2012

So much has happened! After I left KFC I went to explore this park, and I ran into these two guys from Switzerland that I talked to earlier because they saw that I was a tourist and asked me where I was staying, so I hung out with them for the rest of the day and it was really fun. They were hilarious and nice. Felix and Manuel. We went to this open-air music festival and it was sweet.

Then Friday night we went to Club A, a cool club in the city, and I drank WAY too much and threw up throughout the night and they had to take care of me. I talked to this Romanian guy that was really excited to talk to someone from America. We ended up getting back to the hostel at around six a.m. because I couldn't walk until then. And I made Manuel and Felix hold my hands, haha.

Last night we walked to Carrefour and bought pizza and watched football back at the hostel. And smoked a joint with this Italian guy because it was his birthday at midnight. It was so funny, he was like, "What time is it?" and Felix was like, "12:15," and the guy was like, "It's my birthday!" And we all laughed so hard because it was so random and funny.

Today I am leaving for Brasov, but it is raining really hard so I'm waiting for it to stop before I walk to the station. Manuel and Felix already left so I said goodbye to them. I will miss them; they were so nice to me. Most guys are sarcastic and insincere and not fun to hang out with, or else make it too obvious that they just want to fuck me, like that Nigerian guy, but they were not like that. They were so genuine I feel like, and I could talk to them seriously and they would listen. It was cool.

And there was never any weird sexual tension; they didn't seem to think about that at all, and I LOVE that! It was refreshing to not have to deal with the typical male mindset. And at the same time I felt like I could be "one of the guys," you know? Like part of the group and not a burden or anything. I dunno, it was just really nice.

Traveling has been amazing. I have met really great people and learned so much from them, and I have gained a lot of confidence in myself. Oh, I forgot to say I never did do the free tour. Oh well. I also finished *We*, the book I was reading. I actually really liked it, quite poetic. Now I am going to read *Slaughterhouse-Five*. I think that is all for now, dunno what else to say. Scheiße.

28 June 2012

Hello from Cluj-Napoca, the main city of Transylvania! I got here last night around 10:30, took the bus, got a bit lost walking to the hostel, but found it eventually and it was fine.

Today I walked around the city, found a nice little park, went to the botanical gardens and this fucking MASSIVE cemetery which was really cool. This morning I had coffee from the hostel, and it was so strong that I just felt horrible and weird and uncomfortable all day…

I started a new book because I finished *Slaughterhouse-Five* on the train yesterday. It's called *Indecision* and I like it a lot. I liked *Slaughterhouse-Five*, too.

In Brasov I stayed at the Rolling Stone Hostel, and the girl that worked there was funny – Romanian but real good English, short hair, looked a bit like a boy. They had two cats, Judy and Bizza, or Gizza, or something. Brasov was ridiculously beautiful, nestled in the mountains, super green and blue. Crazy.

Right now I'm watching the Italy vs. Germany football game in the kitchen and breakfast area. I dunno what I'll do tomorrow, probably wander around like I usually do. Okay, that is all, I suppose.

29 June 2012

Today I slept in, sort of. I woke around 8:30 because the fucking annoying dog outside would not stop barking. I figured out my life a bit and then went back to bed until noon. Then I walked up this hill, went to the grocery store, walked everywhere, took a nap, and got money out of an ATM to pay the hostel. I had to change rooms because I don't know why, and that kind of really irritated me for some reason. Good thing I leave tomorrow. I'm ready for HUNGARY! I think the train ride is like six hours long. Not cool. Okay, that's all.

Undated

Right now is perfect because I'm sitting by the canal by the black tower and it rained earlier so everything feels lush and ripe. It's cloudy and cool and I'm smoking a cigarette and wearing my flannel, and I bought a kickass bag today in Bran – we took a day trip to Dracula's castle in Bran and to Pelish and Pelishor castles.

I took a nap after and now my hair is messy and bedhead-like. I am giving myself the best vibes ever, I am happy. Last night I was looking through weheartit.com, and I was reminded of all these creative ways to live, so I want to become involved in that website again so I can get ideas and inspiration. Okay, that's all!

02 July 2012

Hello from Budapest! Right now I am sitting in front of the music fountain on Margaret Island. Today I did a free tour; it took so fucking long and wasn't even that cool, but I got good info for things to do and stuff to buy. Like good, cheap wine, which I still need to buy!

Saturday I rode the train all day, and then that night I went to this badass "ruin pub" with these two British guys I met at the hostel. Jack and Doug. It was fun because they were super nice.

The hostel was not particularly hard to find, it's just that there is no way to get in because the door is unmarked and locked and you don't know which doorbell to ring. So I waited there for someone to eventually come by that lived there. It was kind of stupid. But the hostel itself is way cool. There are posters everywhere for this art festival called Hanna-Hanna.

Yesterday I just walked around everywhere and explored a bit randomly. That night was the Eurocup final – Spain vs. Italy. Spain won 4-0, holy shit. They had TV screens in Erzsebet Park and I went there for a bit and there were SO MANY people. Cool. Then the sun went down and I walked along the Danube and it was ridiculously beautiful. Huge buildings lit up and their reflections shining in the river. No words to express.

And so soon I will have to leave this place, and it's weird to think how small these moments are, though thrilling and drowning in beauty and pleasure. It's wonderful, ephemeral. Well, that's all for now, folks.

04 July 2012!

Happy Independence Day!

06 July 2012

Holy shit my life is fucking crazy and amazing. And I love it. So much has happened.

The night of the fourth I became friends with these two Belgian guys: Dragan and Antoine. Then we drank with four British people from my room, one Swedish guy with sweet tats but who was not particularly attractive, and this tall, skinny American guy. And we all went out together, except the Belgian guys and I left the group and had a threesome instead. And it was INCREDIBLE. Haha! So funny. We fooled around in this random park and got kicked out by the police, and then we jumped a fence to fool around and hide.

I had sex with Dragan, who I thought was more attractive. He kind of looked like Ronan from the guys' soccer team in Seattle, but with a Mexican stache. Ha. So because of that we never made it to the club… Eventually Antoine left us, and then Dragan and I had sex again outside the hostel on the balcony/stairs.

Then the next night we all drank again – this was last night – but the Belgians went somewhere else, so I hooked up with one of the British guys, Richard, who was really polite and posh and typical British, but also hilarious and badass. And he had the hugest dick ever. We fucked in the middle of a street/alley and were completely naked, and like five people walked by and totally saw us. But I dunno, they pretended not to notice, I guess. OMG.

Then we did it by Parliament, on the right side underneath a statue. So awesome. He slept in my bed and we petted and fondled each other. We never made it to the club. But we did go to Szimpla, the ruin pub, and there are some hilarious drunken pictures of us. So great. I never remember how it starts, like how I begin to make out with someone, or who makes the first move.

Oh, also, I lost my passport in the cab on the way to the club, and today I went to the US embassy and they had it! It was so crazy, such good luck. The cab driver brought it in.

Then today I took the train to Bratislava, three hours, and I felt hot and sick and horrible. The hostel was a bit hard to find but I got here eventually and I like it a lot. More British guys; they went on a pub crawl tonight and I stayed here. I feel bloated and fat and gross. And tired.

Tomorrow I want to do a free tour! Other than that I have no idea. I think that is all for now!

07 July 2012

Sweat, smoke, thin dresses, losing things, finding things, breeze and darker overcast skies, ruffles fluttering in the wind, a balcony with a bench, flowers, an ash tray, how this slightly reminds me of another world, maybe a dream world, making a connection between neurons, TVs behind windows and blinds, soft laughter, a twitch in your eye, balancing a cigarette lightly between your lips, good posture, eating random things that sound tasty in the moment but never real meals,

dainty, frilly, delicate, poised, balanced and rhythmic, the word "loquacious," staring off into the distance, inside your own mind and a different world, the soles of your feet dirty from walking barefoot, mechanical pencils, clouds that are pink and orange and ready to burst, ripe with the sun's descent, waiting in queues, rushing to finish something when you're late, leaving it unfinished,

08 July 2012

Tomorrow I leave for Vienna. I'm going to be Couchsurfing and my host lives fairly close to the city center, so that is good. Hostels are quite expensive!

Today I walked across the bridge over the Danube and took a nap and took pics of this weird church that looked like it was designed by Dalí. I have also figured out all the places I want to visit in Vienna and figured my life out.

Yesterday I wandered around the Old Town. It's quite touristy but that's okay.

Now it's around 10 p.m. and I've just finished smoking my second to last cigarette and am writing in near darkness but for the light in the common room. I've realized that I'm going to need a new diary soon. Hopefully I will find a cool one in Vienna. I suppose that is all…

09 July 2012

Tired. Made it to Vienna, my host is so cool. There are four or five people that live in the flat but now only my host and one other guy are there. They are both really interesting and cool without being arrogant or pretentious or intimidating. And the flat is SO COOL. Artistic.

I can't concentrate. I'm tired from walking in the super touristy area. It's madness. It's cloudy and a cool breeze. I bought loose-leaf tobacco and rolling paper or whatever the fuck you call it. I think I'm angry right now because I went to Forever 21 and I hate thinking about buying stuff. I don't know why I go there because I don't want any more things. I guess I just got bored. I dunno. I don't want to write anymore right now. Bleh.

10 July 2012

Today is Jenna's birthday. I'm in a Starbucks. Today I woke around 10:30, ate two croissants with jam and cheese, and organized my life a bit before leaving. I walked to a random market that wasn't that interesting, and then to the store Be a Good Girl, which was expensive and did not have any cool journals, which was why I went there to begin with. But I did end up finding a five-euro journal at a different store; the cover is a map of Amsterdam. Just in time, too. Then I bought a 99-cent ice cream at Spar. 500 grams! So delicious and cheap. I dunno what I'm going to do now. Probably just rest here for a while.

Last night Jackie's (my host) friend Dani came over for dinner, which was so delicious. She doesn't shave her legs or wear a bra, and I thought she was cool. She talked a lot about the school system in Europe and politics in Austria. She is 28. And very knowledgeable it seemed. She is going to print off pages of "German for foreigners" for me.

Oh, I rolled two cigarettes and they were awful. But I looked up on YouTube how to do it and I am determined to learn. I think I should only smoke cigarettes I roll. It's cheaper that way!

11 July 2012

Yesterday I went to sleep at five p.m., intending to take a nap, and instead woke up today at 10:30 a.m. I think that's about 17 hours of sleep. I don't know why, but I was so fucking tired yesterday! Today I felt better. Coffee in the morning while chatting with Jackie.

Then I walked to Karlsplatz through Stephansplatz where the huge church is. I walked along the river and took pics of the numerous graffiti on the walls. I also went to the park by the flat, it's called the Augarten, and I read some of *The Dharma Bums* there.

I rolled a ton of cigarettes. I think I'm getting better but I don't know. I also just finished watching *The Runaways* with Kristen Stewart and Dakota Fanning. I really liked it! I think that's all for now. I like this new diary a lot!

15 July 2012

Much has happened. Currently I am in McDonald's. I ate a snack wrap and small fries. I think I'm going to get an iced coffee as well.

I am in Ljubljana, Slovenia. My hosts are two girls in university, and they are so nice and fun to hang out with. Katja and Eva. There is also an American guy named Kris staying there, too. He is pretty weird, loves metal and talks a lot and is kind of annoying.

The first night I was here was Friday, and we went to this badass place, like a graffiti-covered square with bars and clubs all around it. And I got soooo drunk with this red wine I bought for 1.15 euros, and then on Saturday I had a hangover so I slept all day and didn't really do anything.

Around seven p.m. Katja and I walked to the main square and met Eva, and I got a falafel for 80 cents!! I used Katja's student discount and my mind is still blown. It was fucking delicious, too. Then I went to bed semi-early, and today I got up, drank coffee, and then left to explore on my own. Which is good because I needed alone time.

It was raining earlier today, and now it's overcast and cool, which is nice. Right now I am kind of angry/irritated because I had to wait at McDonald's for forever because they are fucking slow and dumb. And then when I was sitting down and writing a family came and totally invaded my space, so I left. And, I dunno, the vibes in McDonald's are not particularly good for writing and thinking. A lot of tourists and such. So, whatever. Everything is closed today because it's Sunday. Maybe this is a good thing.

I am trying to think of what else happened in Vienna. The last night I was there, Bernie, the other roommate, came back and made goulash with stag meat, and it was sooo good! He was cool. I got up at six the next morning to take the train to Italy and it was alright. I was really tired the whole time.

Well, I cannot think of anything else! The last two days in Vienna were overcast and cooler than before, and I am really glad the weather has been like this, because it makes me so tired when it's quite hot.

I keep wanting to write more deep things than just what I have been doing, but once I sit down to write it all leaves me.

God, everyone is so annoying to me right now. People keep getting in my bubble. How do I say, "Get out of my bubble!"? And "Stop staring at me!"?

16 July 2012

Stranded until 7:30 p.m. in Villach, Austria, because the bus I was supposed to take to Venice was full. I'll end up getting there at about midnight now. I am getting things done, though. I'm in another McDonald's. But it's better because I'm upstairs by a window and it's not crowded at all.

I plan on finishing *The Dharma Bums* today. I like it because it makes me less anxious or lonely during my own travels. I like how they love sadness, loneliness, not having all the money or material items in the world. I feel that it is right. The whole aura of the book feels crisp and cold and fresh, like at the top of the ski hill back in Idaho we always went to when the air is so clean that you almost can't breathe. I really want to meet someone like this that I can learn from. And they aren't actually homeless, they just hitchhike from job to job, and spend money wisely and only on things that matter. It's like Sawyer, it really is.* I imagine him encompassing this ideal perfectly.

[*Ana: It isn't, though. Sawyer encompassing this vibe is your projection, because he hitchhiked in Europe that one time. This is the vibe you want, and somehow you've projected it onto Sawyer. Maybe he embodied this vibe for a brief, tiny blip of time, but you've far surpassed him in that respect. –J.]

I am unsure I could hitchhike because I am a girl. But I like the thought of working seasonally or doing temp jobs everywhere and being able to explore and adventure and see all there is in the world. It seems exciting and fulfilling. I love learning new skills, especially skills that enhance survival ability. I love having to adapt to new situations and doing some of the same things along the way. Like writing and reading and jotting down ideas and quotes and desires and such things when they come to mind. I think this is a good way to live. Not the typical nine-to-five hell. Well, I suppose that's all for now.

18 July 2012

HOLY SHIT! So much has happened, I don't even remember when I last wrote. In Venice. The train from Ljubljana left me stranded in Austria, and then when I took the next train to Venice I met these guys from Seattle and drank with them on the train. We got to Venice around midnight and kept drinking, and I ended up staying at their hostel instead of trying to find my way to the campsite, which we all stayed at last night.

I had a foursome with them, only Mason didn't participate. And he was the one I wanted to get with, haha. He has the same mind as me, and is

FUCKING hilarious. There were the Jewish brothers Edward and Justin, who fight all the time and don't look similar at all. And Brayden, who was living and working in Ljubljana and is so ridiculously nice and cool.

Currently I am in a café while they are at a museum. Today Brayden had to go back to Slovenia, and we have just been walking around. Yesterday we explored and drank a lot of alcohol on the canal and met these two people from New York who were really great. They left early this morning, though. I am so happy I made friends with everyone, they are so fun to hang out with.

I wonder what Rome will be like…I leave tomorrow! God, everything has been crazy and I have been getting drunk basically for free because they always buy alcohol and mix it for everyone. God, I am having so much fun. I feel like this is what life is supposed to be like! It's madness and I adore it.

We had a bucket we drank out of and we called it Wilson. Perhaps this is all I have to say. I don't know what else! Ciao!

21 July 2012

I don't even know where to begin. The last night in Venice was a party, as usual. We had dinner with these British girls we met, and it was so funny. They were awesome and hilarious. Lara, Ruby, Katie, and Amanda. Ruby was tiny and talkative and great, and had amazingly thick, luscious eyebrows that I was jealous of. I talked to Lara most of the dinner because Mason was trying to get with Ruby (but ultimately ended up with Lara – AWESOME) and Edward was trying to get with Katie. And Justin was with Amanda at the end of the table, in their own world.

We ended up sleeping at their place, a sweet apartment. The next day we had to get up sort of early and go back to our campsite and check out. I ended up leaving for Rome at 3:30, and I got to my campsite fine. Although it kind of takes forever to get there. And it's nice. Showers kind of smell gross but they are spacious and have hot water. I have a mini cabin to myself, real good. But no wifi in the room; I have to walk all the way up the hill to reception to get wifi and it sucks.

Yesterday I walked all day. Literally. I saw the Colosseum, Pantheon, random other huge crazy buildings, squares, bridges, etc. BUT I lost my wallet…with 10 or 15 euro in it and my debit card. And school ID. Thankfully my hostel has my passport at reception. But it has just fucked everything up. Because when I realized I had lost it I had to run back to where I thought I had left it to see if it was there, talk to the lost and found lady, and then run back to the train so I wouldn't miss it and end up missing the shuttle to camp.

Thankfully I have my other debit card, but I have no clue what the pin number is so I can't get any money! And today is Saturday so the banks closed before I could go to one to see if I could get money without a pin number. Eventually I went to a grocery store and was able to buy food with my card and just sign for it.

Then I tried to take the train to the shuttle, but for unknown reasons it didn't stop at my stop so now I have to wait for an hour until the next train back. Which hopefully will decide to stop for me. And I need to pay the non-English-speaking shuttle driver a euro for the trip, but I don't have one and I can't tell him about my fucked situation because he doesn't speak English!

It has just been a really shitty situation, and living at a campsite far away makes it worse. Ugh. And the whole concept of money is freaking me out and confusing me. And my feet hurt and my shoes are falling apart and my purse is falling apart and I'm so tired all the time, and I'm on my period, and I feel gross because once I was finally able to get food I ate it all (not really all, just a lot).

23 July 2012

Alright. I think I've got everything mostly sorted. I'm at a café by the San Pietro train station, drinking this weird pudding-like chocolate drink. I FINALLY was able to get money from an exchange place. The banks were closed on Saturday and Sunday, and today at four or something, so I missed them. Then I tried to get cash back at a couple places without success. And I was just so fucking frustrated, I just wanted to leave Rome altogether, when I found the exchange place and the universe decided my atonement for all past bad deeds was completed…so yeah.

I was planning on going inside St. Peter's Basilica today because I tried yesterday but my skirt was too short so I couldn't go in, but I just gave up. I just want to get the fuck out of here. I'm sick of Rome and the campsite, and riding the train to get to the campsite.

Yesterday I saw the Spanish Steps and the fountain in front of them, the Pope's Square or whatever it's called, and the Trevi Fountain. SO MANY PEOPLE everywhere! It's madness.

Today after I got money I bought sunglasses and a fedora for five euro total. Awesome. My Hello Kitty sunglasses broke…another way the universe fucked me.

Right now I am at a café with "coffee" and cigarettes, writing, and I really love this vibration. I feel like things will start working out! My life is kind of crazy. I'm in ROME! I'm in Rome…I like to imagine a map of the world and pinpoint where I am, and think about the infinite amount of things I could be doing, and the places I could be, but I am in one tiny place. And I like to think of the places I have been and how I know they exist and are functioning normally, just as I left them, as I am writing this. I love how this thought works around my mind. It's satisfying to me.

I'm thinking more and more about the future, about the things I want to do and where I want to be. I want to publish my book. I want to go to graduate school in a different state. I want to study German in Berlin. I want to work at a hostel. I want to do summer school. I want to make friends in Boise so I'm not bored. I want to buy a longboard and ride it to class. I want to grow my hair super long and wear this fedora and be fashionable and grungy and roll my own cigarettes and read biographies of famous people and watch historical documentaries and learn everything there is to know about the world. I want to work hard so that I deserve the money I make, and I want to be smart with my money and only buy things I need, or absolutely adore.

That's all for now.

26 July 2012

In Torino. I left Rome en route to Pisa, planning on Couchsurfing but my host was MIA, so I stayed at a hostel right by the train station, which was also the cheapest one I could find. It was kind of shitty, though. I slept in a tiny pullout bed, which was really creaky and loud. I watched a movie called *REC^2* about demons, it was alright.

I only stayed for one night in Pisa, and that day I went to the Leaning Tower of Pisa! It was so cool. So many tourists doing that ridiculous pose where it looks like they're holding it up. I smoked cigarettes in the grass and felt good vibrations. Then I left the next morning for Torino, finished a friendship bracelet, started a book called *Underdogs* that I got in Rome for one euro, and just hung out while waiting for my train, which was four hours long and I sat in a cabin with these religious teen boys wearing those long, white dress things with their teachers. It was strange.

I found my hostel alright; it's actually a hotel. I fell asleep at seven intending on taking a nap and instead slept all night. Now I'm at a café drinking an espresso with milk and eating a weird chocolate/cream pastry thing, which is quite good. I was irritated at the Italian coffee, but I think I could get used to espressos if I always get milk to put in it. The vibrations are actually quite nice, especially when you add cigarettes to the equation. And especially when I roll my own cigarettes. And when I'm in Italy outside a café with no tourists, drinking real Italian espressos, being fucking cool, as usual.

The Dharma Bums is the epitome of how I feel I should live my life. I want to travel and work, and change jobs frequently so I will travel continuously. I also like that they have money, but only enough for what they need, like good breakfasts and lots of coffee. It feels really good.

I want to get a tattoo of all the things that give me good vibes, in a list on my left forearm. I wonder how much it would cost. Well, I suppose that is all. I think I will leave now to explore Torino…

27 July 2012

Yesterday I walked ALL DAY. I found a sweet market where I bought one of those espresso maker things like the one my hosts in Vienna had, for three euro! I took tons of pics and saw basically the whole city…

Today I feel is my relaxation day. I am in another café. I ordered a café latte, same as yesterday, but I got a cup of warm milk and a tiny shot of coffee to put into it. What the fuck? I can't get it right! And my guidebook said not to say espresso because that is an English thing and they'll think I'm dumb or something. Fuck it I am ordering an espresso next time. Perhaps they'll know what I mean?

I am sitting right in front of a fan/air conditioner, and I am very happy about it. Perhaps I will stay all day…I think "perhaps" is, like, my fave word. I am going to read my book now, I think.

My book is based in Seattle. 3rd Ave! I loved 3rd Ave. 4th Ave was the public library. This was my life…Melancholy, gray skies, enslavement, wanting to escape, needing to see the people downtown, wanting to be a part of it all, a solitary figure, always solitary, wandering without purpose or goals, willing something to happen, someone to save me, yet it never happened.

29 July 2012

Marseille. It's really windy. Like, everywhere. It's dirty except where all the rich people go. It is a true immigrant city. Loads of people stare at me. Loads of creepers. Not a place to be at night. My hostel's the most expensive hostel I've ever stayed at, and also one of the shittiest. 25 euro a night. The reception guy talks a lot and annoys me, haha.

On the way here the train stopped in Cannes, and I waited for about half an hour for the next train, and it was cool to say I've been to Cannes, although not extensively. I like saying "merci" and "pardon." I try to make my voice sound like Amelie's when I do. People think I'm German when they realize I'm not French. I quite like it. Most of the tourists I've seen appear to be French, rather than American.

Today I wandered, walked by all the boats in the harbor, got a map at an expensive hotel, for free. I also took a nap for a couple hours, and made coffee for the first time in like two weeks, with someone else's milk, ha. It's amazing having a kitchen. Haven't had access to one in ages. I suppose that's all. Au revoir!

01 August 2012

Whoa, August already! I'm in Toulouse sitting on a bench by the river. Toulouse is really nice. Today it's overcast and awesome. The last two nights in Marseille I couldn't sleep, stayed awake until four or five. It sucked. The hostel was quite shitty, and I'm not sure if I liked Marseille that much anyway. Toulouse is great, though!

I took the trains all day yesterday and was tired and gross, so instead of Couchsurfing I just went to a hostel. Which is really cool, there is a kitchen in the room and really close to a grocery store. Thank god. I bought groceries today and it was like America. Hooray! I made instant coffee in my Italian coffee pot thing, and it was revolting until I put lots of milk in it. Hmm…

03 August 2012

In Carcassonne, France waiting for my train to BARCELONA! Yesterday I explored Toulouse a bit but I was so tired for some reason so I took a two-hour nap, and then went to bed at four a.m. last night after watching *Game of Thrones*, which I really like!

The first night in Toulouse I met some people downstairs outside at the tables, just hanging out, and we all went to the little square by the hostel at around 10 p.m. to hang out, drink, listen to music, and people-watch. Tons of interesting people just hanging out.

Today I got up around nine, made espressos!, and got ready to leave, and now I'm here. My train is at five p.m. and it's only 2:45.

11 August 2012

Haven't written in forever. Now I am in Valencia, Spain. Barcelona was CRAZY. The first day I was walking around doing nothing and I met these guys sitting outside a store: Adrien from Argentina who is INSANE – totally covered in tats and obviously fucked up mentally and physically haha, smoking and drinking and yelling and laughing, like, nonstop. Then Mauro from Uruguay who I ended up hooking up with. We had sex on the roof of their tiny badass apartment. It is hard to find, in a labyrinth downtown.

Mauro's bro also lives there, and Mariano, a guy from Argentina who is really nice, and Christina, a black – well, brown – girl, ha. She reminded me of a friendlier Cameron from the soccer team in Seattle. Always rolling joints and not talking very much but nice and not intimidating. I hung out with them and all their friends every day on the beach, and slept in Mauro's bed the first two nights.

The first night we got drunk and high and did MDMA and we went to this Reggae party thing but there weren't very many people there. This guy offered us the MDMA, a white powder from a little plastic baggie he had that you dip your licked finger into. So insane.

The Spanish I learned in high school is coming back a bit and it's so cool. They taught me to say "chupame la poronga," which means "suck my dick" HAHA! OMG they are growing weed in their apartment. Like, legit. A ton of plants in artificial light in this little closet. It's madness. Dunno what else. "The beach is over there!!" We all kept yelling that at everybody, haha.

I am so tired. Valencia is hot and humid. And the beach is too far to walk. I'll be home in Boise in five days. :(Perhaps I'll read my book. Now I am reading *The Windup Girl*. I got it at the hostel in Marseille. Ciao!

Wait, here is a list for you: Starbucks, air conditioning, tired, not hungry but hungry but not, no cash, listless, lethargic, sleepy, nothing at all, to survive is to act in self-interest, wanting my own tiny, shitty apartment in a city by the sea, Lucho as being fucking sexy – the Argentinian friend who had a sleeve and piercings on his left ear and was really skinny, wanting to be creative and make something but having no energy to.

12 August 2012

Tomorrow I leave. Thank god. It's way too hot and humid here. I didn't even leave the hostel today. Just slept and did nothing really. I have felt weird lately. I think it's because I'm supposed to start my period soon. Hope I'm not prego…

I threw away a ton of shit and organized my life and it felt good. Madrid tomorrow, then home. It's going to be so weird and I am afraid I'll forget everything I've learned and come to adopt as my own culture. I don't want to have to check in with my parents all the time or be at home all the time. I really need to make friends…ugh. At least I will be quite busy with school. I hope I will find a boyfriend or something and just sleep at his house all the time. That would be cool. I hope there are people worth meeting at Boise State.

I don't know what else to say, wtf. Ciao!

What I want:

Long hair, long nails with black tips, to smoke in secret and roll my own cigarettes, to have green hair, to be grungy and fashionable, to make friends and drink and do drugs and sleep over with them, to get good grades, to study in coffee shops, to have a job, to make jewelry, to say "ciao," to kiss cheeks, to be bold when it comes to talking to others – to guys, to start conversations, to run and do sit-ups and knee exercises, to drink espressos at cafés and smoke and write,

to have a longboard and go everywhere with it, to wear my black and white Doc Martens all the time, to not have so many things, to purge my bedroom of unwanted items, to smoke in my room and cover it with incense, to watch movies online on the flat-screen TV (hook up my Mac), to eat lollipops, to shop at Hot Topic sometimes, to sell clothes, to imagine all the places I've been and how they exist at every moment, at this moment, to sleep when I'm bored,

to not eat when I'm bored, to make crafts for others, to imagine myself in the eyes of strangers, to read magazines, to watch the news, to never be boring, to rarely use my cell phone, to not have everything perfect and straight and clean, to hang out with the study abroad students at BSU – the foreign ones!, to always be reading a book, to wear my fedora and sunglasses all the time, to smile at people, to initiate conversations, to use military time, to have a pet!

14 August 2012

Outside Starbucks with a Frappuccino. In Madrid! The hostel is cool because it's right next to Plaza España and the metro, and it's cold in there! Ish.

Yesterday I walked around, got money from an exchange place, ate a kebab that was not delicious, bought these sweet green flats at Pimkie that instantly gave me horrible blisters, met some nice British girls, and that's about it, I guess. Met people in the kitchen that were nice.

Today I am going to walk around more, buy food, a postcard for Grandma, hopefully find something for Dad and Sawyer. I think Madrid is a really cool city, and it's not humid, so I like it.

Oh, my digital camera broke again. Lens error shit. Ah, well. I still have film so that is okay. Oh, I bought tobacco and rolling paper, and I found some of the thicker and easier rolling paper! So excited. And my tobacco came with another pack of rolling paper, so WOO!

I am giving myself good vibes: Nirvana shirt, jewelry, fedora, coffee, ashes in the ashtray, it's nice. Perhaps I will go now…

16 August 2012

In Chicago waiting for my flight to Boise. It's eight p.m., but London time is like two a.m., I think. I'm not that tired though, because I slept a ton on the eight-hour plane from London. Window seat = best thing ever.

Yesterday my flight to London from Madrid was at ten p.m. so I went to Starbucks for a while and then hung out with three people from my hostel. A South Korean guy, a Finnish girl that speaks five languages, and a Turkish guy that kind of reminded me of Weston. Fashionable. We went to the Reina Sofia museum and saw Picasso's *Guernica*, which was really cool. I paid six euros for nothing though, because no one checked our tickets. We also walked by the huge pond/lake in the park. And ate at this tapas place where everything was one euro.

Then I went to the airport, drank sangria on the way and got a slight buzz. I slept for four hours on a bench in the airport until taking the bus to Earl's Court in London, then the tube to Piccadilly. I got a sandwich at Café Nero and then took buses around London and felt nostalgic about all the memories of London. And felt sad about leaving, and then met Lina at Piccadilly Circus and had lunch at Starbucks. It was good to see her! Sad to say goodbye.

Then my flight again to Chicago and now I am here. And it's hilarious because I can hear the American accent and it's horrible. Ugh. And there's American football everywhere on TV. At least there are water fountains…haha.

My flight to Boise is three hours. Three hours until I will be home… since one year I've been away! It doesn't feel that long. It feels like a strange dream.

20 August 2012

I've been home for four days! It's weird but normal-ish. Dad was here for the weekend but flew back to Las Vegas last night for work. Mom teared up at the airport when I got here.

Yesterday I did sit-ups for the first time in three or four months, and I'm SO SORE. Tomorrow I'm picking up my Japanese study abroad buddy from the airport, which I volunteered to do through the study abroad program, because since I've studied abroad I know what it's like to not know what's going on at all. On Friday I have an interview for this study abroad job, which I think will be like educating students about what study abroad is like and how it works. I hope I get it! I have to prepare a two to three minute speech. I'm a bit nervous but I know it will be fine.

I fear I will sink back into my old self – be depressed, anxious, insecure. I'm trying to hold on to the memories I've made and the vibes of Europe. I am going to try to be more social and find weird/cool people to be friends with. Hopefully it will work…

I have organized my life a lot in the past four days. Today I ordered a new driver's license and bank card, dropped off a roll of film to get developed, and got a new pin number for my other bank card. I organized my room, got rid of a ton of shit, and am now working on making something artistic with my souvenirs. Whoa.

School starts in a week and I am EXCITED! I don't know what is to come, but I hope it is fun, adventurous, dangerous, sexy, interesting…

27 August 2012

Why can't I write in here more consistently? I am really annoying myself by procrastinating so badly.

Anyway, first day of school! Much has happened. This morning I got up at 9:45 and had coffee and got ready. Then I drove to BSU, got a parking permit, went to the gym and then went to my first class, math at 13:30. It was like 30 minutes long. And I was late so I sat on the floor. Then I parked my car closer to the SUB and now I'm in here waiting for my next class at 16:30. Psych.

This past week I dyed my hair greenish bluish, went on a couple runs, went shopping with Mom, went shopping solo, organized my Europe pics and souvenirs, watched movies from the library…

I hung out with Kenji and Akari, my new Japanese friends! Akari is my buddy, super shy but nice. She got me a Hello Kitty shirt!! Kenji is a boy and I think he's in love with me, ha. I helped them move into their apartments, and the other day we went to a movie with one of Akari's roommates who is a sophomore, really nice, kinda nerdy. Funny. I like her. We met Kenji's roommates after, and a couple of their friends. Drank a bit. Kenji got really drunk but I dunno what happened because I left early. The movie we saw was called *Premium Rush*, with Joseph Gordon-Levitt, who is SEXY. It's about bike messengers in NYC, so tite.

Oh, I also had the interview for the study abroad job. They told me to prepare a two to three minute presentation, and then I didn't even have to do it! They just asked me questions, which weren't too hard to answer. I dunno if they liked me, though…

Well I guess that is all? Perhaps write more later.

29 August 2012

Espresso macchiato, cigarettes, downtown Boise, bicycle, blue hair, Nirvana shirt, loads of jewelry, grungy?, haven't washed my hair in three days, time between classes, writing while smoking, wind = irritating

Want: my own fridge and kitchen and to have single serving size food, and healthy food, to read novels at coffee shops, to have less homework and more free time

"Just because we do bad things doesn't make us bad people." Not sure what that's from but I love this quote, it's so true.

We say we "have to" or "should" do something, and there is not always 100% certainty that we'll do it, so when we don't we get anxious. We expect ourselves to do it but we don't, which leads to cognitive dissonance and anxiety.

04 September 2012

Holy shit what's wrong with me? Haven't written in forever.

Today is Tuesday, I have class in like 45 minutes. I'm at Java sitting on the couch with an iced coffee. I went to the gym earlier and then did math for almost an hour. I'm angry because I hate math, especially the problems that relate it to the real world. I fucking can't do that shit! Also, I feel fat because the blue, silky dress I'm wearing feels almost too small, and I feel sort of uncomfortable. And I'm tired and not looking forward to Biology.

Last night I dyed the top half of my hair purple/light purple. The green faded hella fast and is now more a light turquoise. I bleached my roots before putting in purple.

I am now friends with this guy from Las Vegas named Kyle. He's in this one credit international/foreign language class I'm taking; it's just a ton of international students and people interested in different cultures. We got paired with a South Korean guy. We all hung out last week for the class. Then on Friday I got drunk with Kyle and slept at his apartment. We totally fucked. He's *so* skinny and sort of looks like a little girl, but he has a huge dick. Tats on his leg. He's hilarious. I smoked weed with him, too, and got way too high, but the alcohol canceled it out so I just passed out and didn't have a hangover the next day.

Then on Saturday we went to the market downtown and to this used bookstore where I bought a bio of Courtney Love and a book about Kurt. On Sunday I went on a bike ride downtown with my parents, which was fun. We went to the Co-op and it's so different and terrible. Boring and no personality anymore. Bleh.

Haven't heard back about the job. Dunno if I'll get it. Well, I think perhaps that's all. Dunno…

05 September 2012

I feel weird. Just got out of my foreign language class. I have that nervous feeling like right before a cross-country race in middle school. I hate this feeling! Kyle's making me feel weird because it seems like he feels awkward and doesn't want to talk to me, and it makes me feel bad, sort of. It's stupid because I just want to be friends and hang out but I feel like he thinks I want to be his girlfriend so is trying to not be attached. He's acting like Syler did! When I visited Camila last summer. Holy shit, that is the same exact vibe that I'm getting from Kyle right now. That is so weird.

Okay, well, the only solution is to not text him so he doesn't get the false impression that I'm clingy and want to date him. God, why do guys think this about me? WTF. Because I'm like the exact opposite. Anyway, I don't even know if this is the way he thinks or feels, so I'm just going to stop thinking about this. PROBLEM SOLVED.

10 September 2012

Hello, today's Monday. I'm sitting at a table in the park in front of the capitol. Breezy, shady, warm. I can feel fall coming and I'm excited. Leaves slowly changing. Lovely.

I just got out of Math and it was boring so I read Biology instead. I also went to the gym and rode the bikes and read *The Windup Girl*. I want to finish it soon because I don't like it that much.

Haven't talked to Kyle and I don't really care.

I felt pretty disorganized these past few days, but last night I finished my English journals and essay about why I am in college, so I feel caught up.

Mom and I went to Art in the Park and Saturday market over the weekend, it was fun. And Dad and I saw *The Possession* yesterday at the theatre, it was AWESOME. And I saw all these previews for scary movies that looked really good, so I am excited for all of those.

Dunno what else, my next class is Counseling and then English, which will be long and horrible.

14 September 2012

In the SUB waiting to meet with Omar, my Foreign Language buddy. We get paired up with people and have to like chill with them as homework. It's Friday! I left Math early because I was hating my life. This week I've worked out every day, felt swamped with homework, and…I dunno. Just been super busy. I watch TV at night and do homework, I drink coffee in the morning and listen to music in the car.

Yesterday I was drinking coffee at Dawson's, which is a coffee place downtown, and this guy started talking to me outside the window. He was really pale and had white hair, eyebrows, eyelashes, and weird blue eyes that twitched a lot when he talked. He said I was pretty. Then he invited me to come watch him and his friend do weird flips and stuff in the grass two blocks from the coffee place. So I did for like 10 minutes, and they were really good!

Everyone stares at me lately. This woman in the locker room at the gym said she loved my outfit, that I looked like I came straight from the magazine *Lucky*. It made my day.

There's literally nothing else to say.

16 September 2012

Today is Sunday and I'm anxious for no reason. Mom and I went to the Hyde Park Street Fair and I bought a ring and a bracelet, cool.

Yesterday I slept until one, then went back to bed at two, and finally got up at like four. It was bad. But I went on a run and got some homework done. I was supposed to hang out with Omar later today but I have a lot of English homework and I still feel all anxious and weird. I don't know what to do. I feel kind of angry because I don't want to do anything. God.

I always see these young couples, like teens that have a boyfriend or girlfriend, and I can't figure out why I've never had a boyfriend besides Eli in high school. Even now.* Someone fucking ask me out, it's so annoying to me, Jesus! For some reason this really irritates me. I'm just going to have to initiate shit because guys in the US can't just fucking grow a pair and talk to me. Ugh.

[*Ana: You have the ruler of the seventh conjunct Saturn in the 12th, and your Venus is ruled by Saturn. That's why. Also, why don't you just initiate something? Oh yeah, because no one is good enough. Because Saturn. Lol. –J.]

18 September 2012

Tuesday. I just got done with my first extra credit counseling session, and it was way good. It's for my Counseling class, and I always thought maybe I needed a therapist/counselor, so I decided to do it. The lady was way nice, and I talked about Europe, my life now, and how I think everything is boring.

I dunno what else, I'm in the SUB waiting to go to Bio lecture. I guess that's all…

21 September 2012

What I want: the guy with the dreads in my Eastern Philosophy class,… friends…, a pet, good posture, clean air or a gas mask, grungy clothes and smoking cigarettes and never eating and growing thin and pale, to live on the coast in a shack, to live outside of America, to know everything, to initiate conversations, to be hit on by guys that I actually find attractive, to be the lead singer of Metric,

to have friends that live downtown that would let me sleep over at their flat, for things to be like the movies, it was always like the movies in Europe, (but it's all perspective, I do realize this), to meet people interested in art and creation, to not have to take classes that are pointless for me, to be fashionable and sophisticated in a homeless kind of way, to be lean and toned, maybe that's all for now. Oh, to never be tired or need sleep.

02 October 2012

I can't seem to write on a daily basis, or any basis, actually. It's Tuesday, just got done with my counseling session. She is the nicest person ever. It was my third session? I've decided to keep doing them because I think it's good for me. We only had to do a few for extra credit but we have the option to keep doing them for free because the lady is doing her master's and needs the practice.

Dunno what else. Been running, started watching *Game of Thrones* again…Homework, homework all the days.

03 October 2012

How I feel about the group Coffee and Conversation: I like it, but I just feel jealous that everyone can speak more than one language. And, I dunno. I feel like I'm not a part of it, but I am because I'm there…I guess I could be a true part of it if I keep going and meet a ton of people…I dunno.

I also decided that I don't like Kyle because he's so fucking weird and avoidant. And I just don't like his vibes I decided…

05 October 2012

The artist is a collector, imposter, thief, liar, insomniac, genius, gatekeeper, and half-crazed overlord. The artist is a secret keeper. The artist is immortal.

Pay attention to the voice in your head. Listen to it, soak it in. What does that feel like?

ASK FOR HELP! First from someone close to me, then move farther and farther away.

Today I worked out at the gym and played ping-pong with Omar in the SUB. We also bowled. It was fun. Now I'm at Java and going to do homework.

I tried to sell clothes at this place downtown but they aren't buying during their $2 sale, which is happening now…Lame. I am hoping to be more efficient with completing homework…that's all.

08 October 2012

Today is an angry day, one of those days where I hate everyone and need to escape. Yesterday was Sunday, and also an angry day, but it ended okay because I bought canvases at this craft store and I painted all day, listened to music, and collaged. It was an art day, and I hung out in my room and there were super good vibes.

On Saturday Mom and I went shopping everywhere and we spent $900. Haha. It was kind of insane. She bought a TV and DVD player for the back room, which she's turning into a workout room. We both got new running shoes, thank god. I got the same ones I had before but a different colour.

Today I went to the gym but I felt really tired. And I feel fat-ish. I think it's because I am starting the week where I have my *real* period; all last week I had a sort of period, but this week is when I'm supposed to have it according to my pills.

Well, I dunno what else. I think I'm all hormonal and pissed. I'm going to read.

17 October 2012

I am not sure any of these people are real. What is it about a classroom setting that makes people machines?

19 October 2012

[left blank]

26 October 2012

A love poem: I see myself in you, and I see my goals and desires and interests in you, and I sort of want to be you. I wish I were you. Am I so selfish that the only way I could love someone is wanting to be him? Wanting his essence but as my own spirit? If I could become you and be all the vibes I've ever admired, could I be alone forever and be okay? Can one love herself so fully, so truly, that no others are needed?

Perhaps the true question is: What is the nature of love? What does it mean to love someone?

Here are the people I love: Kan, Sawyer, Kurt and Courtney, Damon and Jamie, 2D and Noodle, Zara, my parents (obviously), Sakura.

There may be others. There are many potentials.

Love is: the way people move their hands when they talk, sharing minds, to look at each other without saying anything, to want to know what is in his mind when there is a glazed look, to see a part of yourself in him, to see a part of him in *you*…

You know, it's almost been 10 days.

31 October 2012

So much has happened. I am so inconsistent. Saturday was a Halloween party with Julia and her cousin. Julia is this girl from my Foreign Language class. She studied abroad in Chile while I was studying abroad in London. She is from Oregon and we hit it off and have been hanging out a lot. She has dirty blonde hair, a small stature, and a really soft voice that seems like it almost doesn't fit her face.

The party was at someone's house and then later we went to Mulligan's downtown. I ended up hooking up with Julia's cousin ha ha ha. I stayed the night at her house and the next day I drove Dad to the airport and then went to a party at Marcos' house, the guy from Spain in my Foreign Language class, and a ton of people from our class went. Omar cooked and we ate on the ground with our hands, and smoked hookah and danced, and it was awesome.

I also applied to H&M and I have no idea if I'll get it but I really want to work there.

I've been talking to my counselor and I feel like she is so helpful and I think she's a genius.

I have been losing weight and I think I'm like two pounds away from my before-London weight. I dunno, though. I gained a lot of weight in Europe because I ate so badly. I literally ate, like, exclusively pasta and Nutella. Not together though, haha. Today I am wearing a dress that didn't fit me a couple weeks ago. It is still a bit tight on my boobs but that just means I don't need a bra. Ha ha ha.

I have so much homework. I get to register for spring classes tomorrow and I am not taking too many classes this time, so I think it will be better.

I'll probs have to do the next fall semester if the classes I'll still need aren't available in the summer. FUH.

I have been wondering this: Why do people put themselves down when they meet new people?

What I want to do more: paint, sketchbook, watch *Adventure Time*, read novels, write in here, walk aimlessly downtown and smoke cigarettes, hang out with Julia, go to parties, apply to jobs…

I got a 72 on my last Bio test, and I hate Bio! It is just so boring to me. I can never concentrate and therefore I can't remember anything. Tomorrow I have a Bio lab test and I think I'll do better than a 72. Hopefully. I studied more than for the lecture exam, and the material is easier, I think. Fuck, I don't know.

I want more tattoos. I want to be weird and surreal and strangely beautiful and graceful. I want to take a dance class, I want to live at the top of a tall building in a shitty apartment with a cuddly dog and the ocean in the distance. I need a beach but a colder beach and the sound of the waves and misty mornings and misty nights and a gray world forever.

02 November 2012

About to study with Julia! It's Friday, I skipped my first class and slept in, went to Math but it got out early. Then I played pool and ping-pong with Yao, my new Foreign Language buddy, and we went to Flying M and did homework for a while.

I took my Bio test, didn't seem too bad. Hopefully I got an A or B. I dunno what else. I hope tonight I'll get a shit-ton of stuff done.

07 November 2012

Coldish air and a cigarette in the air, tall socks but I'm thinking I'll give them to Goodwill, Urban Outfitters, fake rich fashion plastic hipsters. You know plastic is horrible for the environment, yes? Coffee's been tasting bad lately. I skipped my class because I can't sit around anymore, I do not like school anymore. No one will speak up; they're all insecure. I don't speak up either, though…

Coldish air feels so good, it makes everything soothed, my brain is clearing, but it was foggy with my cigarette air. I did it on purpose, though. Maybe I'll ride my bike back to school, I'm just so tired and I can't think, and I need to be creative but I can't think and I'm so tired. That's all for now…

07 November 2012
[same day, different entry]

Yesterday was Election Day, Obama is president again! So excited. I watched it between *The Fifth Element* while doing the stepper.

So much to say. Friday Julia and I got drunk after homework. I didn't get much done because I was too busy talking to these Couchsurfing guys that were also at Goldy's! They were cool. I added one of the guys on CS. Then we went to the bars and this really attractive guy hit on me, his name was Josh? James? Can't remember. He kept saying, "Why do you hate me?" and "FALSE." And he couldn't remember my name. I think he was super fucked up. Shoulda got his number though, he was sexy.

Then on Saturday I did the stepper and homework and read at Goldy's until Julia texted me back, and then we got super drunk at Pengilly's with her friend Nicole and these two Venezuelan guys who taught me to say "I want to fuck you" in Spanish: Te quiero coger. Ha! I got way too drunk after drinking a "Purple Viking" and threw up, and they ended up having to take care of me. And I slept on the guys' couch. All day Sunday I felt super shitty and hungover, and slept and watched TV.

Yesterday I slept all day, voted, went to my counselor who told me that I wiggle my foot more when I am talking about myself. It's because I get nervous-ish when I talk about myself. I dunno.

Tomorrow Julia and I are going to Fatty's to dance to techno music, which I think will be really fun.

I wish I could write in here with more consistency, but I don't think that'll ever happen.

I think Julia and I are becoming good friends, and I think it's crazy. And awesome.

My counselor is so helpful, it blows my mind.

Dunno what else. Been so busy with homework, it's unfortunate. H&M never contacted me so I don't think I got the job. That was one place I would have really liked to work. Oh well, something else will come along.

My computer is on the fritz right now, it's pissing me the fuck off.

Oh! I also registered for classes on Thursday. I won't have class on Monday or Friday, and I am going to take an online class. I hope it turns out well. I am not taking as many credits as I am now, so it will be way better, I already know.

16 November 2012

At the airport about to fly to Seattle to visit Sawyer and Lacy! Much has happened. Techno night at Fatty's was cool, they played The Prodigy, which was badass. We went to Pie Hole afterwards and talked to this guy that I thought was so cool. He had a book with him about meditation called Kundira? I can't remember what it was really called.*

[*Ana: I think it was Kundalini. –J.]

Julia and I picked up her brother Craig from the airport and he and Derek, her cousin that I hooked up with on Halloween, went to Fatty's with us.

On Friday I did homework, I think, and on Saturday we went to Pengilly's, and Omar came with us! He brought a couple friends and it was so fun. We went to Roddy's later and danced and got really drunk, it was awesome. I met this guy named Beau that I had met at the study abroad thing at the beginning of the year, and we made out. And smoked cigarettes outside. He is so attractive. But I ditched him because I didn't want to go with him when they were leaving. I think they were leaving…

Anyway, it was awesome, and I spent the night at Julia's and slept on the floor with her brother. He kept saying, "I love you, I'll take care of you forever, will you be my girlfriend?" It was hilarious. I cleaned up his chicken and orange juice mess in the kitchen and felt very responsible. He is pretty cute, we didn't have sex, though. Good thing!

The next morning Julia had to work at Whole Foods super early, so I went to breakfast with her whole family without her. It was awesome. Her dad drove Craig, Derek, and I to 13th Street Grill in Hyde Park, and he was so funny the whole way there. He kept trying to clean the console and didn't know where to park when we got there. Just awesome.

On Sunday there was another party at Marcos' house, and it was super fun. Craig and Derek came, and Julia made pizza. Then I took my parents to the airport on Monday. Mom is staying in Nevada for Thanksgiving with Dad. This whole week I've been alone at my house. I skipped a lot of school this week, did a lot of homework, have been hanging out with Julia. I love her. We did homework at Goldy's and drank mimosas and it was fun.

I also went to my counselor on Thursday and talked about Chadwick for the first time, in depth, and I cried a little bit. It was cathartic I think. It's weird. My counselor is so helpful to me. I love her, she's such a good person.

Anyway, I'm gonna go!

26 November 2012

Home from Seattle. Holy mother of god it was awesome.

Today is Monday, I skipped Math because I woke up late. I had a test for Counseling which I think went alright, and I'm going to go late to English because I hate it. Yesterday I did a ton of homework, FINALLY finished my existential essay. I dunno how I felt about it. Also, Dad was here so we went to the new James Bond movie, *Skyfall*. It was fucking awesome. Daniel Craig is SEXY.

I hung out with Eli Saturday night because he was home, so that was really cool. The Friday I got into Seattle I lost my phone at the airport, so I don't have a phone anymore. That night Lacy and Sawyer and I went to a few bars in Capitol Hill and Fremont. We had unicorn jizz at the Unicorn, and it was super sugary and later I threw up because of it. And then I was super hungover all the next day and slept a lot.

I walked downtown from their flat and went to Starbucks and did homework. And I got to see Mila, Claire, Mariah, and Calvin that day. Oh, and Tabby too! It was sweet. I also did homework in Fremont with Mila and Mariah the next day.

For Thanksgiving we went to Lacy's mom's house and I met her brother and his girlfriend and Lacy's stepdad. And Curtis the cat! I played "plugging" with him, where you play fetch with earplugs. He loves earplugs. I also played with their husky dog and their other cat named Linus.

Then last Friday we went downtown to watch the Thanksgiving parade, and started drinking at 11 a.m. We walked around Pike's and also did a bit of shopping downtown. We went to this restaurant in Pike's and drank and hung out, and then that night we went to a few bars in Fremont and hung out with these two guys I made friends with. They were awesome and I ditched Sawyer and Lacy later to smoke weed with them at Gasworks and then I slept in their little boat.

I fooled around with one of them, Ramon, who does massage and is half Mexican and has braces and is really cute. And we eventually had sex. He is amazing with his hands…and his mouth, haha. The next day

Ramon and I got coffee and he drove me to Sawyer's flat, and then I had to go to the airport. It was so much fucking fun, I love those guys.

Well, I guess that's all, I'm in a rush to get to class!

30 November 2012

Drinking a double espresso on campus. It cost $1.06 at Einstein Brothers, cheapest espresso ever! Today is Friday, I went to both of my classes but left Math early.

Yesterday I took a Bio test and got a 75, which I thought was good, and a Math test because when I tried to take it on Wednesday my computer got fucked up. I got a 100! Today I also finished all the topics on the computer program we use for Math and completed my six hours for this week. Now I only need to do a few reviews, which I'll do next week, probably.

On Wednesday Julia and I got drunk with Nicole and we went to the Space Bar, which was pretty cool. They don't serve hard alcohol, though. We talked to the bartender and he was nice and cool.

Then we went to the Bistro and met the guy Julia's been hooking up with lately, Jared, and a couple of his friends…and I HATED them. They put me in a bad mood and I was just pissed off. This week I am on my real period (even though I've been on my period for almost two weeks now because my birth control is all fucked up) so I think I was also PMSing and that's part of the reason I was angry.

Julia and I agreed that Jared is immature and he reminds us of high school and pointless drama, and his friends suck, too. That night I slept in my car in the parking lot of this smoothie shop that Julia works part-time at because I was too drunk to drive.

I dunno what else. I feel like I've been getting so much shit done lately and it's the best thing ever. I'm so excited for this semester to end forever.

Good things lately: outfits with favorite, worn-in clothes and no desire to buy new clothes, hand-me-downs from Lacy, double espresso, new glasses that look like the past or some intellectual European man, Julia, getting homework done, magazines and getting them in the mail and collages and perfume scent samples, double espressos that are insanely delicious, anticipation of getting a new camera for Christmas, overcast skies so the whole day feels timeless or at the moment when you wake a bit early and it's not very bright outside, reading novels, bullshitting English papers, thinking I could write a book because the book I am reading is a "National Bestseller" and is written by a teenager in the first person, well, I mean the narrator is a teen in the first person, and I think my book could be just as good…not biting my nails, not being attracted to anyone, I think this is all…

Want to do: paint, sketchbook, make a section in my closet of favorite clothes ever, sell clothes, apply to jobs!

Oh, I also forgot to say that yesterday I saw one of my cousins from Dad's side on campus and I didn't know it was him until he came up to me. And it was crazy and we talked for a bit, and I decided I really like him. I got his phone number so when I get a phone I will text him or something. Weird.

Well, I think this is all for now. I want to start writing in here more often, hopefully I'll have time!

30 December 2012

OMG I haven't written for exactly one month. I've been so ridiculously busy. First I will say that Christmas was great, I got the Finnish backpack I wanted and the coolest digital camera ever that has toy camera setting and lots of other cool stuff. I also got running tights, a running skirt, and stuff for traveling, like an Argentina guidebook! I've been talking to Mauro, the Uruguayan guy I hooked up with in Barcelona, and I think I might visit him in Uruguay and travel around South America. So excite.

Sawyer and Lacy left this morning – they came for Christmas – and my parents just left for REI, so I'm alone. I've really needed to be alone lately. We went skiing for two days in a row and I was so pissed the first day for no reason. I just don't love skiing and my family gets mad at me for it. Then the next day I basically told Mom that she treats me like a child, so she gave me the silent treatment, and I think she's still mad at me.

I finished school a couple weeks ago…finals weren't super stressful. I was worried about my Eastern Phil class and I don't think I did bad. I am so fucking HAPPY I'm done with that semester. Fucking bullshit for like three months, it was killing me.

Oh, I also got a four-week-long job at the university bookstore! It starts January third. Hopefully I will meet cool peeps. It's just during the super busy period when everyone is buying books for the new semester.

I want to take a Spanish placement test and take classes over the summer and next fall, and then get the fuck out of here! "Here" being America. I really need to get a job, too. So I can pay to get the fuck out of here. I also need to pay off my student loans. Ugh.

Oh, I finally introduced Eli and Julia; they hooked up but didn't have sex. Hahaha I am an evil genius.

I got a French press for Christmas and I'm drinking coffee I made with it. Delicious! Pretty strong when you do it right.

I guess that's all for now, dunno why I can't write more consistently.

if you enjoyed this book

If you enjoyed this book I would love your feedback in the form of a short review or some stars on whichever platform you accessed it. **Your comments are extremely appreciated, and will help me out on my indie author career path!!**

If you'd like to read my present musings, please sign up for my newsletter called *Nothing I Say is True: Open Letters to Void* at my website https://jguzman.space/ under the "Correspondence" tab. You can also follow me on Instagram @jguzmanwriter.

Printed in the USA
CPSIA information can be obtained
at www.ICGtesting.com
LVHW021733141023
760737LV00010B/6